healthy
salads

healthy salads

Reader's
Digest

Contents

Mixed salad greens with avocado, page 59

Salads for health

Salads are a healthy choice for all seasons. Year-round, there's a great variety of fresh vegetables and salad greens available. Putting together combinations of colours and textures that taste delicious, look attractive and are good for you is an easy and rewarding thing to do. Salads are so full of flavour and beneficial nutrients and the recipes in this book contain less than 30 g total fat and a maximum of 8 g saturated fat per serving.

Essential nutrients

Salads provide an easy, delicious way to enjoy a wide variety of foods and a wide variety of essential nutrients. All kinds of fruits and vegetables can be included and, because they are mostly used raw, or are only briefly cooked, they retain the maximum amount of vitamins and minerals.

For example, the vitamin C content of raw vegetables and fruit is higher than that of cooked. An added benefit is that raw foods take longer to chew and also take longer for the system to digest, which can help to curb the urge to overeat. Starchy carbohydrates, such as rice, potatoes, pasta, grains and bread are filling, and are easy to incorporate into salads. Also, by adding moderate amounts of protein-rich food, such as meat, chicken, fish, nuts or eggs, a salad can be turned into a well-balanced main dish.

Reap the benefits

A salad you've made yourself has the big advantage in that you know exactly what's in it, right down to the last grain of salt. Salad greens, raw or cooked vegetables, crunchy grains, different types of pasta, fresh berries, citrus fruits, hard-boiled eggs, nuts, rice, soft and hard cheeses, meat, poultry and fresh or canned fish – you can draw on all these to make a salad.

Research indicates that eating at least five servings of vegetables and fruit each day provides a wide range of nutrients required for good health. Regularly incorporating salads into your diet is a simple way to achieve that goal and obtain sufficient vitamins, phytochemicals, fibre and minerals. The ideal is to choose servings according to the traffic light principle. Every day you should eat at least one serving of red fruit or vegetables (such as capsicums, tomatoes and strawberries), at least one of yellow or orange (carrots, yellow squash, melon, pineapple or oranges), as well as at least one of green (broccoli, beans, spinach, salad greens, peas, watercress or kiwifruit). Follow this formula and you will include the broadest possible range of nutrients in your diet.

Salad greens at a glance

There is a large variety of lettuce types and salad greens to choose from all year round, with new varieties appearing regularly in the marketplace. Visit your local farmers' market to look for new ones that your supermarket or vegetable shop may not yet stock.

Salad greens

● **BABY SPINACH** Glossy green spinach leaves have a slight metallic taste because of their iron content. The iron is not all absorbed by the body, however, due to the leaf's oxalic acid content. Spinach does contain many other valuable nutrients, especially antioxidants and bioflavonoids that may help block cancer-causing substances and processes. Use raw baby spinach leaves in salads for the best flavour.

DRESSING A simple olive oil and vinegar dressing with a few drops of walnut oil.

● **BOK CHOY** This leafy, dark green vegetable is a variety of Chinese cabbage. Also known as pak choy, its taste resembles Swiss chard. For salads, add raw chopped leaves and stems cut into thin strips.

DRESSING An Asian-style dressing including hot and spicy ingredients such as chilies and soy sauce, as well as crushed garlic and finely chopped fresh ginger.

● **BUTTER LETTUCE** Green and also red butter (butterhead) lettuces are among the most popular varieties. They form small heads with soft, tender leaves. The heart is tender and the leaves have a mild flavour. Do not cut the large, floppy outside leaves; just tear them into bite-sized pieces.

DRESSING A light herb vinaigrette or a yogurt or sour cream dressing.

● **COS LETTUCE (ROMAINE)** This long, oval head of fairly tightly packed leaves has sturdy, rich green outer leaves and crisp white ribs. It has a mild, tangy flavour. Cos lettuce contains carotenoids and is rich in potassium.
DRESSING A vinaigrette with finely chopped hard-boiled eggs or crumbled feta cheese.

● **CRESS AND SPROUTS** Mustard cress is a mixture of seedlings of garden cress and white mustard (or sometimes rape). The very delicate shoots taste peppery. They, like alfalfa or mung bean sprouts, are often used as a garnish, and also add plenty of texture to salads.
DRESSING A classic vinaigrette with a few drops of hazelnut or sesame oil.

● **CURLY ENDIVE** This is also known as frisée lettuce. The large, slightly flattened round head has thin, light green leaves with wavy edges tapering to fine points. They have a bitter taste. The paler, greenish-yellow leaves at the centre form a compact heart. They are milder and more tender than the outer ones.
DRESSING Thousand Island dressing and cream or sour cream dressings.

● **ICEBERG LETTUCE** A large, round, tightly packed lettuce that looks like a type of cabbage, iceberg has pale green leaves with a bland but refreshing taste. This lettuce is useful more for its crunch than its taste.
DRESSING The mild taste works with all types.

● **LAMB'S LETTUCE** Also known as mâche, corn salad or field salad, this lettuce is comprised of small rosettes of pretty, delicate, mid-green leaves. They have a velvety texture and a mild flavour. Young leaves are the sweetest. Lamb's lettuce is high in beta carotene, which is thought to help fight heart disease and certain types of cancers.
DRESSING Classic vinaigrettes using fruit vinegars, such as raspberry vinegar, and a few drops of walnut oil combined with olive oil.

● **LOLLO ROSSA AND LOLLO BIONDA** These two Italian relatives of the butter (butterhead) lettuce form compact leaf rosettes without a firm head. They look very frilly because the ends of the reddish dark copper or light green leaves are finely crinkled, with lacy edges. The crisp aromatic leaves are more robust than those of butter lettuce and will last a little longer.

DRESSING A classic vinaigrette of good-quality olive oil and balsamic vinegar.

● **MIGNONETTE (BIBB)** A loose-head lettuce, the mignonette has small, soft, mild-tasting leaves with ruffled edges. It is available in red and green varieties which look attractive mixed together in a salad. Because it is a loose-head lettuce with no firm core, the leaves are easy to pick individually.

DRESSING Cream dressing with herbs.

● **NASTURTIUMS** This plant with its bright orange, red and yellow blossoms looks attractive in mixed green salads and fruit salads. Wash flowers carefully and avoid any that have been sprayed with herbicides. Flowers vary in taste from peppery to virtually tasteless and are valued more for their appearance than for their flavour.

DRESSING All types of dressings.

● **OAK LEAF LETTUCE** The leaf shape gives this lettuce its name. Oak leaf is a loose-head lettuce with thin, tender reddish-brown or green scalloped leaves. They have a mild nutty flavour that teams well with mushroom or meat salads.

DRESSING Stronger vinaigrettes with red wine vinegar or specialty vinegars such as cassis vinegar.

● **RADICCHIO** A member of the endive (chicory) family, radicchio is a tight head of crisp leaves that are a vibrant red or reddish-purple with white veins. They have a bitter, nutty taste that teams well with citrus fruits. Treviso is a variety of radicchio with long, elongated leaves and a slightly milder flavour. Radicchio is high in beta carotene and other cancer-fighting phytochemicals.

DRESSING A robust dressing, such as one containing mustard or blue cheese.

● **ROCKET** Also known as arugula, rocket (which is also termed a herb) is made up of clumps of rounded and spiked tender leaves that jut out from slender stems. Their distinctive peppery taste becomes more pronounced as the plant ages. Rocket goes well with tomatoes, feta, Parmesan, olives and roasted, marinated vegetables.

DRESSING Classic vinaigrette containing balsamic vinegar and a little lemon juice.

● **SORREL** The elongated dark green leaves of sorrel resemble those of spinach but are more oval or spear-shaped. They have a pronounced sharp, lemony taste. Slice leaves into thin strips and use sparingly in combination with milder salad greens or other wild herbs or the taste can be overpowering. Use in white fish or salmon salads.

DRESSING A mild dressing made with cream cheese or a more robust blue cheese.

● **WITLOF** Also known as Belgian endive or chicory, this is a bullet-shaped head of smooth, compact, white to pale yellow leaves. The pale tones are the result of the plant not being exposed to sunlight during its growth. Crisp and succulent, witlof leaves have a bitter taste that works well in egg salads or ones that contain citrus fruits or celery.

DRESSING A garlicky or herb dressing.

Herbs for salads

A handful of finely chopped fresh parsley, a tablespoon of chopped chives or a scattering of tarragon leaves gives salads that extra layer of flavour. Ideally, use fresh herbs in salads. They're best purchased as and when needed because they do not keep well for more than a few days. If you have the space, it's very rewarding to grow your own. When a recipe calls for dried herbs, remember that they are much stronger in flavour than fresh. They will keep their flavour for longer if stored in cool, dark, tightly sealed containers. Excellent herbs to add to salads are basil, chives, coriander (cilantro), dill, lemongrass, marjoram, mint, parsley, rocket (arugula), rosemary, tarragon, thyme and watercress.

Salad dressings

HERB DRESSINGS

Herb dressings look attractive and go well with many types of salads such as green or vegetable salads and also with pasta or rice salads, fish or meat salads. To maximise their flavour, it's a good idea to make them in advance and store them in the refrigerator for a day or two. Taste and add more chopped fresh herbs just before serving. It's fun to make your own herb vinegars or oils and they will make your herb dressings even better.

Basic vinaigrette

This recipe makes about 150 ml (5 fl oz). Add herbs as desired.

120 ml (4 fl oz) extra virgin olive oil
2 tablespoons red wine vinegar
1 teaspoon Dijon mustard or wholegrain mustard
pinch of caster (superfine) sugar (optional)
salt and pepper

Whisk all the ingredients together in a bowl, or shake in a screw-top jar, adding salt and pepper to taste. Use immediately or refrigerate in a jar until needed.

Raspberry nut herb vinaigrette

These flavours complement bitter radicchio or peppery rocket (arugula) leaves.

2 teaspoons hazelnut oil
3 tablespoons canola or peanut oil
2 tablespoons raspberry or other fruit vinegar
1 tablespoon Dijon mustard
salt and ground white pepper
2 spring onions (scallions), finely chopped
4 sprigs each parsley, tarragon, basil and dill

Whisk the two oils with the vinegar, mustard, salt and pepper. Add spring onions and finely chopped leaves of all the herbs.

Classic herb vinaigrette

Excellent with green salads and vegetable salads as well as grain or rice salads.

3 tablespoons white wine, sherry, or herb vinegar, or lemon juice
1 teaspoon Dijon or herb mustard
salt or herb salt and ground white pepper
4 tablespoons good-quality olive oil
5 small sprigs each parsley and dill
small bunch of chives
2 sprigs each marjoram and basil
pinch of sugar

Whisk vinegar, mustard, salt and white pepper in a bowl until salt has dissolved. Add olive oil, whisking until vinaigrette is slightly creamy. Chop herb leaves finely and stir into vinaigrette. Add sugar and more salt and pepper, to taste.

Lemon thyme vinaigrette

A refreshing vinaigrette to use with green and vegetable salads, chicken, beef or seafood salads.

4 tablespoons olive oil
2 tablespoons lemon juice
1 teaspoon Dijon mustard
4 lemon segments, peel and pith removed
salt and ground white pepper
pinch of sugar
½ teaspoon grated lemon rind
½ teaspoon chopped fresh lemon thyme leaves

Combine olive oil, lemon juice and mustard in a bowl. Beat vigorously with a whisk. Chop lemon segments coarsely; whisk into vinaigrette. Season with salt, white pepper and sugar. Stir in lemon peel and lemon thyme.

CREAMY SAUCE CLASSICS

Mayonnaise-style sauces that form a coating over salad ingredients are suitable for potato or pasta salads. Thin them with a little yogurt or milk for delicious green or vegetable salads. Some of these sauces are based on an egg yolk and oil combination. The eggs should be very fresh. (If you do not want to use raw eggs, buy good-quality mayonnaise in a jar.) The oil can be a neutral-tasting one such as canola or peanut oil or a full-bodied olive oil. For the best result, use ingredients at room temperature.

Roquefort dressing

This tangy dressing goes well with mixed bean, green or vegetable salads.

50 g (2 oz) Roquefort or Gorgonzola cheese
½ cup (125 g/4 oz) crème fraîche or light sour cream
2 tablespoons white wine vinegar
3 tablespoons fresh orange juice
1 tablespoon walnut oil
salt and freshly ground black pepper, to taste
generous pinch of sugar
3 tablespoons coarsely chopped walnuts, optional

Mash cheese finely with a fork in a bowl. Add crème fraîche and stir to make a smooth, creamy mixture. Add vinegar, orange juice and walnut oil and mix well. Add salt, pepper and sugar, to taste. Stir in chopped walnuts, if using.

Garlic sauce (aïoli)

Goes with potato, meat or salmon or white fish salads.

1 large slice white bread, crust removed
2 to 3 tablespoons milk
3 cloves garlic, roughly chopped
1 teaspoon salt
2 medium very fresh egg yolks
1 cup (250 ml/8 fl oz) olive oil
1 tablespoon lemon juice
freshly ground black pepper
4 tablespoons yogurt, optional

Tear bread into small pieces; drizzle with milk. Mix to a fine paste with garlic and salt. Using an electric whisk, add egg yolks and 2 tablespoons oil. Whisk in lemon juice, then another 2 tablespoons oil, drop by drop. Add remaining oil in a thin, steady stream; stir constantly. Add salt and pepper. Add yogurt, if using.

Thousand island dressing

Particularly good with fish and seafood salads. This is a very easy, quick recipe.

1 cup good-quality mayonnaise
½ cup (125 ml/4 fl oz) chili sauce or tomato sauce (ketchup)
few drops Tabasco (optional)
2 tablespoons chopped pimiento-stuffed olives
2 tablespoons finely chopped green capsicum (bell pepper)
1 tablespoon finely chopped white onion
1 teaspoon finely chopped pimiento
salt and freshly ground black pepper

Combine the ingredients and refrigerate. Add salt and pepper just before serving.

Classic mayonnaise

Perfect for potato salads. Spices or herbs can be added.

2 medium very fresh egg yolks
1 teaspoon Dijon mustard
2 tablespoons white wine vinegar or
    lemon juice
1 cup (250 ml/8 fl oz) olive oil
salt and freshly ground white pepper

Whisk egg yolks, mustard and vinegar in a medium bowl. Using an electric whisk, add oil, first drop by drop, then in a slow, steady stream. (If mixture curdles or splits, add a little hot water and beat vigorously.) Add salt and white pepper to taste. Refrigerate 1 to 2 days.

Basic creamy dressing

Rich and smooth, lower in fat than mayonnaise-based dressings.

120 ml (4 fl oz) fromage frais or Greek-style yogurt
1 tablespoon lemon juice
2 tablespoons white wine vinegar
pinch of caster (superfine) sugar
salt

Put all the ingredients into a bowl, adding salt to taste, and stir together until evenly blended. Taste and add more sugar, salt or lemon juice, if necessary. Cover the bowl with plastic cling film and keep in the refrigerator until ready to use. It can be stored in the refrigerator for 1 to 2 days.

CAESAR SALAD

COBB SALAD

THREE BEAN SALAD

POTATO SALAD WITH BACON

COLESLAW

CUCUMBERS WITH DILL AND
SOUR CREAM DRESSING

TEX MEX SALAD

Classic salads

BOCCONCINI, BASIL AND TOMATOES

ITALIAN BREAD SALAD

FRESH TOMATO SALAD

RUSSIAN SALAD

MIDDLE EASTERN BREAD SALAD

ROASTED BEETROOT AND ORANGE SALAD

TABOULEH

GREEK SALAD

THAI BEEF SALAD WITH PEANUTS

GADO GADO

Caesar salad

Serves 4   Preparation 30 minutes

2 small heads cos (romaine) lettuce
4 large leaves iceberg lettuce
50 g (2 oz) Parmesan, in a piece
2 slices sourdough bread, crusts removed
1 tablespoon olive oil

ANCHOVY DRESSING
4 anchovy fillets
1 clove garlic, roughly chopped
4 tablespoons olive oil
1 very fresh large egg yolk
2 tablespoons lemon juice
2 tablespoons Dijon mustard
1 tablespoon Worcestershire sauce
pinch of sugar
salt and freshly ground black pepper

1 Cut cos and iceberg lettuce leaves into bite-sized pieces. Use a vegetable peeler or cheese grater to shave Parmesan into thin slivers.

2 To make anchovy dressing, place anchovy fillets and garlic in a bowl and mash to a paste. Whisk in olive oil, egg yolk, lemon juice, mustard, Worcestershire sauce and sugar. Add salt and freshly ground black pepper, to taste.

3 To make croutons, cut bread into small cubes. Heat olive oil in a large nonstick pan over medium heat. Add bread cubes; cook until golden brown on all sides, taking care they do not burn. Set aside; keep warm.

4 Arrange lettuce leaves and shaved Parmesan on individual serving plates. Drizzle dressing over salad and sprinkle on bread cubes.

PER SERVING kilojoules 1554, protein 12 g, total fat 30 g, saturated fat 6 g, carbohydrate 14 g, fibre 6 g, cholesterol 68 mg

Cobb salad

Serves **6**   Preparation **20 minutes**   Cooking **15 minutes**

2 cups (500 ml/16 fl oz) chicken stock
½ cup (125 ml/4 fl oz) dry white wine
1 small lemon, chopped
4 skinless chicken breast fillets (about 600 g/1 lb 8 oz in total)
4 rashers (slices) bacon, trimmed of fat and chopped
3 medium eggs, hard-boiled, chopped
1 small head red mignonette (bibb) lettuce
2 cups trimmed watercress
3 medium tomatoes (about 500 g/1 lb), chopped
1 large avocado, diced
75 g (2 oz) blue cheese, crumbled

VINAIGRETTE
2 tablespoons olive oil
1 tablespoon white wine vinegar
2 teaspoons finely chopped tarragon
1 teaspoon Dijon mustard
1 teaspoon honey
1 clove garlic, crushed
salt and freshly ground black pepper

1 Combine stock, wine and lemon in a medium saucepan; bring to a boil. Reduce heat; add chicken. Simmer, covered, about 15 minutes or until cooked through. Drain chicken; cut into bite-sized pieces. Leave to cool.

2 Cook bacon in a frying pan over high heat until crisp. Drain on paper towels.

3 Tear lettuce leaves into small pieces. Arrange lettuce and watercress on individual serving plates and top with chicken, bacon, eggs, tomatoes, avocado and cheese.

4 To make vinaigrette, whisk oil, vinegar, tarragon, mustard, honey and garlic until combined. Add salt and pepper to taste. Drizzle salad with vinaigrette.

PER SERVING kilojoules 1811, protein 37 g, total fat 28 g, saturated fat 8 g, carbohydrate 5 g, fibre 4 g, cholesterol 189 mg

Three bean salad

Serves **4**   Preparation **10 minutes**   Cooking **7 minutes**

300 g (10 oz) green beans, trimmed, halved
1 can (400 g/14 oz) red kidney beans, rinsed and drained
1 can (400 g/14 oz) cannellini or lima beans, rinsed and drained
1 small red onion, finely chopped
2 large tomatoes (about 350 g/12 oz), seeded and chopped
3 tablespoons chopped fresh flat-leaf parsley
3 tablespoons olive oil
2 tablespoons lemon juice
1 clove garlic, crushed
salt and freshly ground black pepper

1 Half fill a medium saucepan with water and bring to a boil. Add green beans; cook 5 to 7 minutes or until just tender. Drain; rinse with cold water.

2 Combine green beans, kidney beans, cannellini beans, onion, tomatoes and parsley in a serving bowl. Mix oil, lemon juice and garlic. Add salt and pepper to taste. Stir into salad.

PER SERVING kilojoules 1046, protein 10 g, total fat 15 g, saturated fat 2 g, carbohydrate 19 g, fibre 11 g, cholesterol 0 mg

Potato salad with bacon

Serves 4   Preparation 10 minutes   Cooking 15 minutes

1 kg (2 lb) small new potatoes (chats)
5 rashers (slices) bacon, trimmed of fat and chopped
4 medium eggs, hard-boiled, quartered
¼ cup (50 g/2 oz) chopped pickled cucumbers
3 tablespoons chopped fresh flat-leaf parsley
⅔ cup (150 g/5 oz) low-fat mayonnaise
4 tablespoons light sour cream
1 tablespoon lemon juice
1 teaspoon ground sweet paprika
2 tablespoons chopped fresh dill

1 Half fill a large saucepan with water; add potatoes and bring to a boil. Reduce heat to a simmer, cook 10 to 12 minutes or until just tender. Drain and cut in half.

2 Cook bacon in a lightly oiled frying pan over high heat or in the microwave, until crisp. Drain on paper towels.

3 Place warm potatoes in a large serving bowl; add eggs, pickled cucumbers and parsley; toss gently.

4 Combine mayonnaise, sour cream, lemon juice and paprika in a small bowl. Add to salad and toss gently. Sprinkle bacon and dill on top.

PER SERVING kilojoules 1858, protein 25 g, total fat 19 g, saturated fat 7 g, carbohydrate 42 g, fibre 6g, cholesterol 239 mg

Coleslaw

½ head medium savoy (green) cabbage (about 500 g/1 lb)
1 large carrot, grated
½ small onion, finely chopped
3 spring onions (scallions), thinly sliced
2 celery stalks, thinly sliced
3 tablespoons chopped fresh flat-leaf parsley
½ cup (125 g/4 oz) good-quality mayonnaise
2 teaspoons lemon juice
1 teaspoon Dijon mustard
salt and freshly ground black pepper

1 Finely shred the cabbage using a sharp knife, a mandoline slicer or a food processor.

2 Place cabbage in a large bowl with carrot, onion, spring onions, celery and parsley; toss to combine.

3 Whisk mayonnaise, lemon juice and mustard in a small bowl until well combined. Add salt and pepper to taste. Add dressing to salad; toss gently to combine.

PER SERVING kilojoules 595, protein 3 g, total fat 10 g, saturated fat 1 g, carbohydrate 12 g, fibre 6 g, cholesterol 8 mg

Cucumbers with dill and sour cream dressing

Serves **4**   Preparation **50 minutes including chilling**

2 large telegraph (English) cucumbers (about 500g/1 lb)
1 teaspoon salt
1 small red onion, thinly sliced
3 tablespoons chopped fresh dill

SOUR CREAM DRESSING
½ cup (125 g/4 oz) sour cream
2 tablespoons white wine vinegar
1 teaspoon sugar
2 teaspoons Dijon mustard
salt and freshly ground black pepper

1 Cut cucumbers in half lengthwise and scoop out seeds with a small spoon. Slice flesh thinly. Place cucumbers in a colander and sprinkle with salt. Let stand 15 minutes.

2 Rinse under cold water to remove excess salt; drain. Place cucumbers, onion and dill in a large bowl. Cover and refrigerate at least 30 minutes.

3 To make sour cream dressing, whisk sour cream, vinegar, sugar and mustard until combined. Add salt and pepper to taste. Spoon over cucumbers, onion and dill; toss gently to coat.

PER SERVING kilojoules 604, protein 3 g, total fat 13 g, saturated fat 8 g, carbohydrate 5 g, fibre 2 g, cholesterol 41 mg

Tex mex salad

Serves **4**   Preparation **20 minutes**   Cooking **15 minutes**

2 skinless chicken breast fillets (about 300 g/10 oz in total)
1 tablespoon vegetable oil
3 tablespoons enchilada sauce from a jar
4 large corn tortillas
1 large head cos (romaine) lettuce
1 can (400 g/14 oz) red kidney beans, rinsed and drained
1 large avocado, diced
2 tablespoons chopped pickled jalapeños (hot chilies)
2 sprigs fresh flat-leaf parsley, for garnish

PICO DE GALLO
2 large tomatoes (about 350 g/12 oz), seeded, chopped
1 small red onion, finely chopped
1 fresh small red chili, finely chopped
3 tablespoons chopped fresh coriander (cilantro)
2 tablespoons vegetable oil
2 tablespoons lime juice
1 clove garlic, crushed

1 Preheat grill (broiler) or barbecue to medium hot.

2 Brush chicken with half the oil; cook 5 minutes each side or until cooked through. Leave 5 minutes; slice thinly.

3 Bring enchilada sauce to a boil in a medium saucepan; add chicken and toss to coat. Remove from heat and cover to keep warm.

4 Brush tortillas with remaining oil; cook on barbecue grill plate (rack) about 2 minutes each side or until browned lightly and crisp. Break into large pieces.

5 To make pico de gallo, combine tomatoes, onion, chili and coriander in a small bowl; add combined oil, lime juice and garlic and toss to combine.

6 Chop or tear lettuce leaves into small pieces. Arrange lettuce on a large serving platter. Top with beans, avocado, pickled jalapeños and pico de gallo. Arrange chicken on top and sprinkle with tortilla pieces. Garnish with parsley.

PER SERVING kilojoules 2066, protein 27 g, total fat 30 g, saturated fat 5 g, carbohydrate 30 g, fibre 11 g, cholesterol 50 mg

Bocconcini, basil and tomatoes

Serves **4**   Preparation **15 minutes**

300 g (10 oz) drained baby bocconcini, cut in half
500 g (1 lb) cherry tomatoes, cut in half
½ cup (80 g/3 oz) black olives
2 tablespoons chopped fresh flat-leaf parsley
12 fresh basil leaves
2 teaspoons olive oil
salt and freshly ground black pepper

1 Place bocconcini, tomatoes and olives in a serving bowl.

2 Sprinkle on parsley and basil. Drizzle salad with olive oil and add salt and pepper to taste. Toss gently to combine.

PER SERVING kilojoules 878, protein 14 g, total fat 14 g, saturated fat 8 g, carbohydrate 7 g, fibre 2 g, cholesterol 26 mg

Italian bread salad

300 g (10 oz) day-old ciabatta
1 large red onion, diced
2 medium tomatoes, diced
2 stalks celery, diced
2 Lebanese (Mediterranean) cucumbers, diced
3 sprigs oregano
4 tablespoons finely chopped fresh basil leaves
4 tablespoons olive oil
salt and coarsely ground black pepper
3 tablespoons good-quality red wine vinegar

1 Cut bread into large pieces and moisten with a little water. Soak briefly, squeeze to remove liquid, then tear into small pieces. Mix bread, onion, tomatoes, celery and cucumbers in a serving bowl.

2 Finely chop oregano leaves. Mix with basil, oil, salt and pepper. Pour over bread and vegetables. Chill, covered, about 1 hour. Stir in red wine vinegar. Season to taste.

PER SERVING kilojoules 1572, protein 8 g, total fat 20 g, saturated fat 3 g, carbohydrate 39 g, fibre 5 g, cholesterol 0 mg

Fresh tomato salad

Serves 4   Preparation 40 minutes including standing

3 medium tomatoes (about 500 g/1 lb)
4 spring onions (scallions), finely sliced
½ cup (30 g/1 oz) chopped fresh coriander (cilantro) leaves
3 tablespoons chopped fresh mint leaves
2 small red chilies, seeds removed, finely chopped
½ teaspoon ground coriander
½ teaspoon ground cumin
3 tablespoons lime juice
salt and freshly ground black pepper

1 Cut tomatoes in half, remove seeds and dice flesh. Place in a serving bowl with spring onions, coriander, mint, chilies, ground coriander, cumin and lime juice. Stir to combine.

2 Leave for 30 minutes to allow the flavours to develop. Taste just before serving, adding salt and freshly ground black pepper to taste.

PER SERVING kilojoules 124, protein 2 g, total fat 0.5 g, saturated fat 0 g, carbohydrate 4 g, fibre 3 g, cholesterol 0 mg

Russian salad

Serves **4**   Preparation **15 minutes**   Cooking **30 to 35 minutes**

500 g (1 lb) beetroot (beets), trimmed
500 g (1 lb) potatoes, peeled, cut into wedges
½ cup (60 g/2 oz) frozen peas
3 tablespoons sliced dill pickles (cucumbers)
1 small red onion, finely sliced
3 tablespoons good-quality mayonnaise
3 tablespoons sour cream
2 teaspoons white wine vinegar
1 teaspoon Dijon mustard

1 Half fill a large saucepan with water; add beetroot and bring to a boil. Cook 20 to 25 minutes or until just tender. Drain and cool. Peel; cut into wedges.

2 Half fill a medium saucepan with water; add potatoes and bring to a boil. Cook 8 minutes; add peas. Cook another 2 minutes or until vegetables are tender. Drain.

3 Combine beetroot, potatoes and peas in a large bowl; add pickles and onion. Whisk mayonnaise, sour cream, vinegar and mustard in a small bowl until smooth. Add to salad; toss gently to combine.

PER SERVING kilojoules 913, protein 5 g, total fat 11 g, saturated fat 4 g, carbohydrate 25 g, fibre 5 g, cholesterol 24 mg

Middle eastern bread salad

Serves **6**   Preparation **20 minutes**   Cooking **5 minutes**

1 telegraph (English) cucumber, seeded and diced
3 medium tomatoes, seeded and diced
    (cubes should be about the same size as the cucumber)
6 spring onions (scallions), finely chopped
salt and freshly ground black pepper
1 small iceberg lettuce, roughly chopped
3 small rounds pita bread
2 tablespoons olive oil

DRESSING
4 tablespoons olive oil
grated peel and juice of 1 lemon
2 cloves garlic, crushed
2 tablespoons roughly chopped fresh flat-leaf parsley
2 tablespoons roughly chopped fresh mint leaves
2 tablespoons roughly chopped fresh coriander (cilantro) leaves

1 Combine cucumber, tomatoes and spring onions in a colander and sprinkle
with salt. Leave 10 minutes to drain. Place in a serving bowl with lettuce.

2 Roughly tear pita bread into small pieces. Heat oil in a frying pan. Fry bread
over medium heat until golden brown. Drain on paper towels to remove excess oil.

3 To make dressing, whisk all ingredients together until combined. Drizzle over
salad; toss well to coat. Season with salt and pepper. Top with pieces of fried pita
bread just before serving.

**PER SERVING kilojoules 945, protein 4 g, total fat 16 g, saturated fat 2 g,
carbohydrate 16 g, fibre 4 g, cholesterol 0 mg**

Roasted beetroot and orange salad

Serves 4   Preparation 10 minutes   Cooking 45 minutes

800 g (1 lb 12 oz) baby beetroot (beets), trimmed and scrubbed
3 cloves garlic, peeled, flattened with the back of a knife
2 tablespoons olive oil
1 large orange
⅔ cup (100 g/4 oz) black olives
1 small red onion, thinly sliced
250 g (8 oz) rocket (arugula)
2 teaspoons red wine vinegar
1 teaspoon whole-grain mustard
salt and freshly ground black pepper

1 Preheat oven to 180°C/350°F. Combine beetroot, garlic and oil in a baking dish. Cover with foil and roast 45 minutes or until beetroot is tender. Remove beetroot from dish; reserve pan juices.

2 Cut cooked beetroot into quarters. Peel and segment orange. Place in a serving bowl with the olives, onion and rocket.

3 Combine vinegar, mustard and reserved pan juices in a small bowl. Season to taste with salt and pepper. Stir into salad just before serving.

PER SERVING kilojoules 758, protein 4 g, total fat 10 g, saturated fat 1 g, carbohydrate 19 g, fibre 5 g, cholesterol 0 mg

Tabouleh

Serves 4   Preparation 15 minutes plus 45 minutes standing

1 cup (180 g/7 oz) instant burghul (bulgur wheat) or couscous
2 medium tomatoes, finely diced
3 Lebanese (Mediterranean) cucumbers, finely diced
4 spring onions (scallions), sliced
2 cups (about 125 g/4 oz) finely chopped fresh flat-leaf parsley
1½ cups (about 75 g/3 oz) finely chopped fresh mint
4 tablespoons olive oil
6 tablespoons lemon juice
salt and freshly ground black pepper
cos (romaine) lettuce leaves, for serving
1 heart cos (romaine) lettuce, cut into strips
mint and coriander sprigs, for garnish
1 large tomato, cut into wedges, for garnish

1 Place burghul in a pan with 2 cups (500 ml/16 fl oz) water. Bring to a boil. Remove from heat; leave 20 minutes to absorb liquid. Fluff with a fork.

2 Combine burghul, tomatoes, cucumbers, spring onions, parsley and mint in a bowl. Whisk oil and 4 tablespoons lemon juice; add salt and pepper to taste. Pour over salad and toss to combine; leave 30 minutes.

3 Arrange lettuce leaves on a large platter. Season tabouleh to taste with salt and remaining 2 tablespoons lemon juice; fold in lettuce strips. Arrange on lettuce leaves. Garnish with herb sprigs and tomato wedges.

PER SERVING kilojoules 1485, protein 9 g, total fat 20 g, saturated fat 3 g, carbohydrate 34 g, fibre 12 g, cholesterol 0 mg

Greek salad

Serves **4**   Preparation **20 minutes**

3 medium tomatoes
3 small Lebanese (Mediterranean) cucumbers
2 large red onions
2 medium green capsicums (bell peppers)
⅔ cup (100 g/4 oz) black olives
100 g (4 oz) pickled mild or hot chilies
3 tablespoons olive oil
2 tablespoons red wine vinegar
salt and freshly ground black pepper
150 g (5 oz) feta cheese
1 teaspoon dried oregano or 2 teaspoons fresh oregano leaves

1 Cut tomatoes into wedges. Cut cucumbers into thick slices. Slice onions, not too thinly. Cut capsicums into strips.

2 Place all the vegetables in a bowl. Top with olives and pickled chilies. To make vinaigrette, whisk 2 tablespoons oil and all the vinegar until combined; add salt and pepper to taste. Drizzle over salad.

3 Cut feta into thick cubes or crumble coarsely; add to salad. Sprinkle oregano on top and drizzle with remaining 1 tablespoon oil.

PER SERVING kilojoules 1543, protein 11 g, total fat 28 g, saturated fat 14 g, carbohydrate 19 g, fibre 4 g, cholesterol 26 mg

Thai beef salad with peanuts

Serves 4   Preparation 20 minutes   Cooking 10 minutes

3-cm (1-inch) piece fresh ginger root
4 sprigs coriander (cilantro)
500 g (1 lb) beef fillet
4 tablespoons sunflower oil
3 tablespoons lime juice
2 tablespoons soy sauce
½ teaspoon ground ginger
⅓ cup (50 g/2 oz) unsalted peanuts
2 medium red onions, thinly sliced
salt
2 spring onions (scallions)
1 fresh red chili
1 Lebanese (Mediterranean) cucumber, thinly sliced, for garnish
few mint sprigs, for garnish

1 Peel ginger and chop finely. Chop coriander leaves finely. Cut beef into very thin strips.

2 Heat oil in a wok or deep frying pan. Sear meat on all sides over high heat, stirring, until no more juice escapes. Place in a bowl. Mix lime juice, soy sauce, ground ginger and fresh ginger and add to meat, stirring to combine.

3 Wipe wok or pan with paper towels. Dry-roast peanuts lightly over medium heat; add to meat. Stir red onions and coriander into meat. Season with salt.

4 Slice pale green and white parts of spring onions on the diagonal. Cut chili in half, remove seeds. Cut into fine strips.

5 Spoon salad onto individual plates. Sprinkle with spring onions and chili strips. Garnish with cucumber slices and mint leaves.

PER SERVING kilojoules 1759, protein 29 g, total fat 30 g, saturated fat 6 g, carbohydrate 7 g, fibre 2 g, cholesterol 66 mg

Gado gado

Serves 6   Preparation 30 minutes   Cooking 15 minutes

1 small head iceberg lettuce, leaves
separated
2 large potatoes, boiled and sliced
200 g (7 oz) green beans, sliced,
blanched
¾ cup (80 g/3 oz) bean sprouts,
blanched
1½ cups (125 g/4 oz) shredded
Chinese (napa) cabbage, blanched
2 medium tomatoes, cut into wedges
1 medium red onion, sliced
3 spring onions (scallions), cut in
short lengths
1 Lebanese (Mediterranean)
cucumber, thinly sliced
2 fresh red chilies, seeded and thinly
sliced
4 medium hard-boiled eggs, sliced
125 g (4 oz) fried tofu (bean curd), cut
into cubes

PEANUT SAUCE
½ cup (125 ml/4 fl oz) vegetable oil
1¼ cups (200 g/7 oz) raw unsalted
peanuts
2 cloves garlic, chopped
4 spring onions (scallions), chopped
salt
½ teaspoon chili powder
1 teaspoon soft brown sugar
1 tablespoon dark soy sauce
2 cups (500 ml/16 fl oz) water
juice of 1 lemon

1 Arrange lettuce leaves on a large plate. Add all the remaining salad ingredients
in small groups (for people to help themselves). Serve peanut sauce separately.

2 To make peanut sauce, heat oil in a wok or frying pan over high heat. Stir-fry
peanuts until light golden brown, about 4 minutes. Remove with a slotted spoon
and place on paper towels to cool. Pound or process peanuts until finely ground.
Discard oil from pan, reserving 1 tablespoon.

3 Crush garlic and spring onions in a mortar and pestle with a little salt. Fry in
reserved oil, about 1 minute. Add chili powder, sugar, soy sauce and water. Bring
to a boil; add ground peanuts. Simmer, stirring occasionally, until sauce is thick,
about 10 minutes. Add lemon juice and more salt, if needed. Cool. (Sauce can be
made ahead and stored in a jar in the refrigerator for up to 1 week.)

**PER SERVING kilojoules 1597, protein 18 g, total fat 27 g, saturated fat 4 g,
carbohydrate 17 g, fibre 9 g, cholesterol 143 mg**

GREEN SALAD WITH CREAMY CHIVE YOGURT

CARROT SALAD

MIXED SALAD GREENS WITH AVOCADO

SNOW PEA AND LETTUCE SALAD

ROOT VEGETABLE SALAD WITH SPICY VINAIGRETTE

MIXED SALAD WITH CAPERBERRIES

ARTICHOKE AND HERB SALAD WITH WHITE BEANS

BEAN SALAD WITH PAPRIKA VINAIGRETTE

Vegetable and green salads

EGGPLANT SALAD WITH TAHINI

EGG AND RADISH SALAD

WARM GRILLED VEGETABLE SALAD

GRILLED TOMATO SALAD

ARTICHOKE AND RADICCHIO SALAD

WATERCRESS AND SPINACH WITH GOAT'S CHEESE

BOK CHOY WITH PAN-FRIED TOFU AND PEANUTS

MIXED MUSHROOM SALAD

TOSSED SALAD WITH PEARS AND BLUE CHEESE

RADICCHIO AND FENNEL SALAD WITH ORANGES

Green salad with creamy chive yogurt

Serves **4**   Preparation **15 minutes**   Cooking **3 to 4 minutes**

3 heads cos (romaine) lettuce
2 spring onions (scallions),
    thinly sliced

VINAIGRETTE
1 tablespoon olive oil
1 tablespoon white wine vinegar
1 tablespoon lemon juice
1 teaspoon Dijon mustard
salt and freshly ground black pepper

CREAMY CHIVE YOGURT
½ cup (125 g/4 oz) light sour cream
3 tablespoons yogurt
½ cup (30 g/1 oz) chopped chives
salt and freshly ground black pepper

CROUTONS
3 thick slices of bread
1 tablespoon butter mashed with
    1 teaspoon chopped fresh basil

1 Chop lettuces into wide strips. Place in a serving bowl.

2 To make vinaigrette, whisk oil, vinegar, lemon juice and mustard until combined; add salt and pepper to taste.

3 To make creamy chive yogurt, combine sour cream, yogurt and chives; add salt and pepper to taste.

4 To make croutons, cut bread into small cubes. Melt herb butter in a nonstick pan over medium heat. Add bread cubes; cook until golden brown on all sides, taking care butter does not burn. Set aside; keep warm.

5 Drizzle vinaigrette over lettuce. Toss to coat. Sprinkle with spring onions. Spoon on creamy chive yogurt dressing; top with croutons.

PER SERVING kilojoules 1166, protein 9 g, total fat 17 g, saturated fat 8 g, carbohydrate 22 g, fibre 8 g, cholesterol 35 mg

Carrot salad

4 medium carrots (about 500 g/1 lb), peeled, cut into matchsticks
¾ cup (60 g/2 oz) fresh flat-leaf parsley leaves
4 tablespoons shredded coconut, toasted
3 tablespoons hazelnuts, toasted, chopped
3 tablespoons sultanas
3 tablespoons olive oil
2 tablespoons orange juice
1 teaspoon ground cumin, toasted

1 Place carrots, parsley, coconut, hazelnuts and sultanas in a medium serving bowl.

2 Combine oil, juice and cumin and stir into salad. Divide salad among individual serving bowls.

PER SERVING kilojoules 1151, protein 3 g, total fat 23 g, saturated fat 6 g, carbohydrate 15 g, fibre 6 g, cholesterol 0 mg

Mixed salad greens with avocado

Serves 4   Preparation 5 minutes

1 tablespoon olive oil
1 tablespoon lemon juice
1 teaspoon Dijon mustard
pinch of salt
350 g (12 oz) mixed salad greens, such as iceberg,
    radicchio and rocket (arugula)
1 medium red onion, thinly sliced
1 large avocado, peeled and diced

1 Whisk oil, lemon juice, mustard and salt in a serving bowl until combined.

2 Add salad greens and red onion. Toss well to coat with dressing. Add avocado; toss to combine.

PER SERVING kilojoules 810, protein 3 g, total fat 19 g, saturated fat 4 g, carbohydrate 5 g, fibre 3 g, cholesterol 0 mg

Snow pea and lettuce salad

Serves **4**   Preparation **20 minutes**   Cooking **5 minutes**

500 g (1 lb) snow peas (mange-tout)
crisp hearts of 2 green lettuces
3 spring onions (scallions), finely sliced
2 tablespoons vegetable oil
2 tablespoons white wine vinegar
salt and freshly ground black pepper
trimmed alfalfa or mung bean sprouts or mustard cress, for garnish
2 thick slices wholegrain bread
1 tablespoon butter
1 clove garlic, peeled, sliced lengthwise

1 Blanch snow peas in lightly salted boiling water 1 minute. Immerse in iced water; drain.

2 Tear lettuce into pieces. Distribute among serving bowls. Add snow peas; sprinkle with spring onions.

3 To make vinaigrette, whisk oil, vinegar and a generous seasoning of salt and pepper. Drizzle over salad greens. Sprinkle with sprouts.

4 To make croutons, cut bread into small cubes. Heat butter in a nonstick frying pan over medium heat. Add garlic, cut surfaces face down. Fry 30 seconds; remove from pan and discard. Place bread cubes in garlic butter; cook until golden brown on all sides, taking care butter does not burn. Serve salad topped with hot croutons.

PER SERVING kilojoules 991, protein 7 g, total fat 16 g, saturated fat 4 g, carbohydrate 16 g, fibre 6 g, cholesterol 12 mg

Root vegetable salad with spicy vinaigrette

Serves **4**   Preparation **1 hour including chilling**   Cooking **1 hour 30 minutes**

600 g (1 lb 8 oz) beetroot (beets)
500 g (1 lb) waxy potatoes
3 medium tomatoes
2 spring onions (scallions), finely
    chopped
2 cloves garlic, finely chopped
½ cup (40 g/2 oz) finely chopped
    fresh flat-leaf parsley
3 sprigs coriander (cilantro),
    leaves finely chopped
⅔ cup (100 g/4 oz) black olives, for
    garnish

SPICY VINAIGRETTE
5 tablespoons white wine vinegar
6 tablespoons olive oil
½ teaspoon salt
pinch of freshly ground black pepper
pinch of cayenne pepper

1 Place beetroot in a large saucepan, cover with water and bring to a boil. Cook 1 hour 30 minutes, or until a fork is easily inserted. Drain, reserving 4 tablespoons cooking water. Refresh under cold running water; leave to cool.

2 Meanwhile, cook potatoes in boiling water 20 to 30 minutes, or until just cooked. Drain, refresh under cold running water; leave to cool. Peel beetroot and potatoes, halve and slice thinly. Place in separate bowls.

3 Plunge tomatoes into boiling water 1 minute. Transfer to a bowl of iced water. Peel tomatoes, cut in halves, remove seeds and dice flesh. Combine tomatoes and spring onions with beetroot. Add garlic, parsley, coriander and reserved cooking water.

4 To make spicy vinaigrette, whisk vinegar, oil, salt, pepper and cayenne pepper until combined. Stir two thirds vinaigrette into beetroot mixture and remainder into potatoes. Cover and refrigerate 30 minutes.

5 Just before serving, add salt, pepper and more vinegar to taste. Spoon beetroot salad onto a platter and arrange potato salad around it. Garnish with olives.

PER SERVING kilojoules 1594, protein 5 g, total fat 28 g, saturated fat 4 g, carbohydrate 27 g, fibre 6 g, cholesterol 0 mg

Mixed salad with caperberries

Serves 4 Preparation 40 minutes including chilling Cooking 20 minutes

800 g (1 lb 12 oz) waxy potatoes
150 g (5 oz) rocket (arugula), roughly chopped
2 medium red onions, finely sliced into rings
200 g (7 oz) cherry tomatoes, halved
½ cup (60 g/2 oz) each pitted green and black olives

CAPERBERRY VINAIGRETTE
2 to 3 tablespoons sherry vinegar
¼ cup (50 g/2 oz) caperberries or capers plus 1 to 2 tablespoons
    brine from the jar
1 teaspoon Dijon mustard
4 tablespoons olive oil
salt and freshly ground black pepper

1 Cook potatoes in boiling salted water for 20 minutes, or until just cooked. Rinse under cold running water. Peel and dice when cool enough to handle. Place potatoes, rocket, onions, tomatoes and olives in a serving bowl.

2 To make caperberry vinaigrette, whisk vinegar, 1 to 2 tablespoons caperberry brine, mustard and oil until combined. Add salt and pepper to taste. Pour vinaigrette over salad and toss gently to combine.

3 Leave salad, covered, in a cool place 30 minutes. Add more salt, pepper and vinegar to taste. Slice caperberries in half and add to salad.

PER SERVING kilojoules 1389, protein 6 g, total fat 19 g, saturated fat 3 g, carbohydrate 34 g, fibre 6 g, cholesterol 0 mg

Artichoke and herb salad with white beans

Serves 4   Preparation 10 minutes   Cooking 5 minutes

4 large globe artichoke hearts (in oil and vinegar, from a jar)
100 g (4 oz) ham, in one piece
4 tablespoons olive oil
2 cloves garlic, finely chopped
4 tablespoons dry white wine
4 sprigs thyme, leaves finely chopped
2 sprigs marjoram, leaves finely chopped
1 sprig rosemary, leaves finely chopped
½ cup (40 g/2 oz) finely chopped fresh flat-leaf parsley
1⅓ cups (250 g/8 oz) drained and rinsed canned white beans
2 roma (plum) tomatoes, sliced
150 g (5 oz) rocket (arugula), torn into small pieces
salt and freshly ground black pepper
2 to 3 tablespoons lemon juice

1 Cut artichoke hearts into even pieces. Cut ham into dice, discarding excess fat.

2 Heat 2 tablespoons oil in a nonstick pan. Add garlic, cook, stirring, just until transparent. Add artichoke pieces and wine. Cook over high heat, covered, about 2 minutes. Add ham and herbs; heat briefly. Set pan aside and let mixture cool until lukewarm. Transfer to a serving bowl.

3 Add beans, tomatoes and rocket to artichoke mixture. Add salt, pepper and remaining lemon juice and oil to taste.

PER SERVING kilojoules 1370, protein 11 g, total fat 25 g, saturated fat 4 g, carbohydrate 13 g, fibre 6 g, cholesterol 13 mg

Bean salad with paprika vinaigrette

Serves 4   Preparation 15 minutes   Cooking 15 minutes

4¼ cups (600 g/1 lb 8 oz) frozen or shelled fresh broad (fava) beans
1 small cucumber
2 shallots, finely diced
3 roma (plum) tomatoes, sliced
1 small red and 1 yellow capsicum (bell pepper), seeded and diced
½ cup (40 g/2 oz) finely chopped fresh flat-leaf parsley

PAPRIKA VINAIGRETTE
4 tablespoons olive oil
2 tablespoons balsamic vinegar
1 tablespoon lemon juice
1 teaspoon ground cumin
½ teaspoon ground sweet paprika
pinch of cayenne pepper
pinch of freshly ground black pepper

1 Place beans in a saucepan. Cover with lightly salted water; bring to a boil. Cook 15 minutes or until crisp-tender. Drain and leave to cool.

2 Cut cucumber in half lengthwise and remove seeds with a teaspoon. Slice cucumber thinly. Combine broad beans, cucumber, shallots and tomatoes in a serving bowl.

3 To make paprika vinaigrette, whisk ingredients until combined.

4 Arrange salad on individual plates. Stir diced capsicums into vinaigrette. Drizzle on salad. Sprinkle with parsley.

PER SERVING kilojoules 1171, protein 12 g, total fat 19 g, saturated fat 3 g, carbohydrate 14 g, fibre 8 g, cholesterol 0 mg

Eggplant salad with tahini

Serves 4   Preparation 1 hour 20 minutes including chilling   Cooking 25 to 30 minutes

2 large eggplants (aubergines) (about 600 g/1 lb 8 oz)
7 tablespoons lemon juice
3 tablespoons tahini (sesame seed paste) from a jar
    plus 1 tablespoon oil from jar
3 cloves garlic, crushed
salt
2 tablespoons pomegranate seeds, for garnish (optional)
chopped fresh parsley, for garnish

1 Preheat oven to 240°C/475°F. Line a baking tray with cooking (aluminum) foil. Wash eggplants; place wet on foil. Bake 25 to 30 minutes, turning occasionally.

2 Rinse eggplants under cold running water. Cut in half, scoop flesh into a bowl and drizzle with 3 tablespoons lemon juice to prevent discolouration.

3 Mash eggplants in a bowl. Mix in tahini and 1 tablespoon oil from the jar, 3 tablespoons lemon juice and the garlic. Cover and refrigerate at least 1 hour.

4 Just before serving, add remaining 1 tablespoon lemon juice and salt to taste. Garnish with pomegranate seeds, if using, and parsley.

PER SERVING kilojoules 714, protein 5 g, total fat 14 g, saturated fat 2 g, carbohydrate 5 g, fibre 6 g, cholesterol 0 mg

Egg and radish salad

Serves **4** Preparation **25 minutes**

2 medium eggs, hard-boiled
8 large curly endive (frisée) lettuce leaves
2 medium heads witlof (Belgian endive/chicory)
2 spring onions (scallions)
16 medium red radishes

CREAM CHEESE DRESSING
100 g (4 oz) cream cheese with herbs or plain cream cheese
3 tablespoons yogurt
2 tablespoons herb vinegar
2 tablespoons canola oil
2 tablespoons finely chopped fresh herbs such as a mixture
    of parsley, chives, dill, chervil or sorrel
salt and freshly ground black pepper

1 Slice eggs into thin rounds. Divide endive among serving plates. Place witlof leaves on top, open sides upwards.

2 Finely chop white part of spring onions; slice green part into thin rounds. Finely dice radishes. Mix with white part of spring onions.

3 To make cream cheese dressing, combine cream cheese, yogurt, vinegar and oil. Add herbs, reserving a little for garnish. Season with salt and pepper.

4 Sprinkle radish/spring onion mixture evenly over the witlof. Top with dressing. Add egg slices. Sprinkle with remaining herbs and green parts of spring onions.

PER SERVING kilojoules 958, protein 7 g, total fat 21 g, saturated fat 7 g, carbohydrate 2 g, fibre 1 g, cholesterol 134 mg

Warm grilled vegetable salad

Serves **4**   Preparation **20 minutes**   Cooking **15 minutes**

500 g (1 lb) green capsicums (bell peppers), seeded and sliced thickly
500 g (1 lb) red capsicums (bell peppers), seeded and sliced thickly
500 g (1 lb) zucchini (courgettes), thinly sliced lengthwise
1 large red onion, cut into wedges
6 baby eggplants (aubergines), thinly sliced lengthwise
150 g (5 oz) portobello or large Swiss brown mushrooms, thickly sliced
3 tablespoons olive oil
1 medium head treviso or round radicchio
1 cup (120 g/4 oz) pitted black olives
2 tablespoons balsamic vinegar
1 tablespoon finely chopped fresh oregano

1 Preheat grill (broiler) or barbecue until medium–hot.

2 Mix capsicums, zucchini, onion, eggplants, mushrooms and 1 tablespoon oil in a large bowl. Cook vegetables on barbecue grill plate until browned and tender, turning occasionally to cook evenly.

3 Place warm vegetables in a serving bowl. Add treviso, olives, vinegar, oregano and remaining 2 tablespoons oil. Toss gently to combine.

PER SERVING kilojoules 1098, protein 9 g, total fat 15 g, saturated fat 2 g, carbohydrate 23 g, fibre 8 g, cholesterol 0 mg

Grilled tomato salad

10 roma (plum) tomatoes, halved lengthwise
2 cloves garlic, finely sliced
150 g (5 oz) rocket (arugula)
¾ cup (90 g/3 oz) pitted green olives

CROUTONS
4 thick slices baguette
3 tablespoons olive oil

VINAIGRETTE
2 tablespoons olive oil
1 tablespoon balsamic vinegar
1 tablespoon lemon juice
salt and freshly ground black pepper

1 Preheat grill (broiler) or barbecue to medium–hot. To grill (broil) tomatoes, place cut-side up on a baking tray. Sprinkle with garlic. Place under grill 2 to 3 minutes. Turn and cook another 2 minutes. To barbecue, place tomatoes cut-side down on a piece of cooking (aluminum) foil. Cook over fire 2 to 3 minutes. Turn; cook another 2 minutes. Tomatoes should still hold their shape.

2 To make croutons, slice bread into small cubes. Heat 3 tablespoons olive oil in a nonstick frying pan over medium heat. Add bread cubes; cook until crisp on all sides. Set aside.

3 Tear rocket into small pieces. Arrange on serving plates.

4 To make vinaigrette, whisk 2 tablespoons olive oil, balsamic vinegar, lemon juice, salt and pepper until combined.

5 Place grilled tomatoes on top of rocket. Drizzle with vinaigrette. Arrange olives and croutons over the top.

PER SERVING kilojoules 1388, protein 5 g, total fat 24 g, saturated fat 3 g, carbohydrate 23 g, fibre 4 g, cholesterol 0 mg

Artichoke and radicchio salad

Serves **4**   Preparation **10 minutes**   Cooking **12 minutes**

4 small globe artichokes
1 clove garlic, thinly sliced
4 tablespoons olive oil
100 ml (4 fl oz) dry white wine
salt and freshly ground black pepper
2 tablespoons balsamic vinegar
3 tablespoons finely chopped fresh flat-leaf parsley
few sprigs lemon thyme, leaves finely chopped
2 medium heads treviso or round radicchio
80 g (3 oz) pecorino cheese
lemon wedges, to serve

1 Use kitchen scissors to trim tips of artichoke leaves. Cut artichokes in half. Scrape out fibrous inner part with a teaspoon. Rinse well to remove any remaining fibre. Cut artichokes into four pieces.

2 Heat oil in a nonstick frying pan with a lid over medium heat. Add artichoke pieces and garlic. Cook, stirring, about 5 minutes. Add wine; season with salt and pepper. Cover pan and cook for about 6 minutes, or until artichokes are crisp-tender.

3 Using a slotted spoon, transfer artichokes to a plate. Leave to cool. Stir vinegar and herbs into pan juices. Cut radicchio into large pieces. Combine raddichio and pan juices and distribute among serving plates.

4 Using a vegetable peeler, slice pecorino into large, thin shavings. Arrange artichokes on top of radicchio. Scatter on pecorino. Serve with lemon wedges.

PER SERVING **kilojoules 1154, protein 10 g, total fat 24 g, saturated fat 6 g, carbohydrate 4 g, fibre 2 g, cholesterol 18 mg**

Watercress and spinach with goat's cheese

Serves **4**   Preparation **15 minutes**   Cooking **15 minutes**

3 slices light rye bread, crusts removed
2 tablespoons butter
1 large clove garlic, halved lengthwise
100 g (4 oz) firm goat's cheese
100 g (4 oz) watercress
100 g (4 oz) baby spinach leaves
1 shallot, finely chopped
2 tablespoons olive oil
2 tablespoons balsamic vinegar
½ teaspoon Dijon mustard
salt and freshly ground black pepper

1 To make croutons, cut bread into small cubes. Melt about 1½ tablespoons butter in a nonstick frying pan over medium heat. Add garlic, sauté 2 minutes; discard. Add bread cubes; cook until golden brown on all sides, taking care butter does not burn. Set aside; keep warm.

2 Slice goat's cheese into four equal pieces. Heat remaining butter in a pan over medium heat. Add cheese; cook until it begins to melt and develops a golden-brown crust, about 4 minutes each side.

3 Divide watercress, spinach and shallot among serving plates. Whisk oil, vinegar, mustard, salt and pepper until combined. Drizzle over salad greens. Place a piece of cheese on each plate and top with croutons.

PER SERVING kilojoules 1204, protein 7 g, total fat 22 g, saturated fat 8 g, carbohydrate 15 g, fibre 3 g, cholesterol 35 mg

Bok choy with pan-fried tofu and peanuts

Serves 4   Preparation 20 minutes   Cooking 5 minutes

2 small heads baby bok choy
2 medium carrots
4 spring onions (scallions)
200 g (7 oz) firm tofu (smoked variety, if available)
2 small red chilies, or to taste
3 tablespoons peanut oil
2 tablespoons lime juice
2 tablespoons soy sauce
¼ teaspoon ground ginger
¼ teaspoon grated lemon peel
pinch of soft brown sugar
salt
3 tablespoons roasted peanuts
1 tablespoon finely chopped fresh coriander (cilantro) leaves, for garnish

1 Cut bok choy into thin strips. Score five narrow grooves lengthwise along each carrot. Slice carrots into thin rounds to create flower-shaped disks.

2 Finely dice white parts of spring onions. Cut green parts into thin rings. Distribute bok choy, carrots and spring onions among serving plates.

3 Cut tofu into small cubes. Halve chilies lengthwise and discard seeds. Dice chilies finely.

4 Whisk 2 tablespoons of the peanut oil, all the lime juice, soy sauce, ground ginger, lemon peel, sugar and a little salt in a bowl until combined. Stir in chilies. Drizzle over salad.

5 Heat remaining 1 tablespoon oil in a nonstick frying pan over medium heat. Add tofu and fry until golden brown on all sides. Add peanuts and cook briefly, stirring. Add tofu and peanuts at once to salad. Sprinkle with coriander and serve.

PER SERVING kilojoules 1022, protein 9 g, total fat 20 g, saturated fat 3 g, carbohydrate 6 g, fibre 4 g, cholesterol 0 mg

Mixed mushroom salad

about 700 g (1 lb 8 oz) button mushrooms, halved
150 g (5 oz) portobello or Swiss brown mushrooms, thickly sliced
150 g (5 oz) oyster mushrooms, chopped
2 cloves garlic, crushed
1 tablespoon fresh thyme leaves
3 tablespoons olive oil
150 g (5 oz) enoki mushrooms
1 medium red onion, sliced thinly
¾ cup (60 g/2 oz) chopped fresh parsley leaves
½ cup (30 g/1 oz) chopped chives
2 tablespoons red wine vinegar
salt and freshly ground black pepper

1 Preheat oven to 200°C/400°F. Mix button, Swiss brown and oyster mushrooms with garlic and thyme in a roasting pan; drizzle with oil. Roast about 20 minutes or until tender. Add enoki mushrooms; roast another 5 minutes.

2 Place warm mushrooms in a large serving bowl; add onion, parsley, chives and vinegar. Add a little salt and a generous amount of pepper. Toss to combine.

PER SERVING kilojoules 853, protein 11 g, total fat 15 g, saturated fat 2 g, carbohydrate 8 g, fibre 10 g, cholesterol 0 mg

Tossed salad with pears and blue cheese

Serves **6**   Preparation **20 minutes**

2 pears, halved, cored and thinly sliced
¾ cup (185 ml/6½ fl oz) buttermilk
1 tablespoon white wine vinegar
salt and freshly ground black pepper
2 tablespoons chives, cut into short pieces
1 head butter (butterhead) lettuce
1 head radicchio or other red lettuce
2 cups (75 g/3 oz) watercress leaves
1 small cucumber, thinly sliced
2 tablespoons crumbled blue cheese

1 In a small bowl, toss pears with 2 tablespoons of the buttermilk to prevent flesh browning. Whisk the remaining buttermilk, the vinegar and a pinch each of salt and pepper in another small bowl until combined. Add chives.

2 Tear or chop leaves of both lettuces. Mix with watercress and cucumber. Arrange on serving plates and top with blue cheese and sliced pears. Drizzle a little buttermilk dressing over the top, serving the remainder separately.

PER SERVING kilojoules 394, protein 4 g, total fat 3 g, saturated fat 2 g, carbohydrate 12 g, fibre 3 g, cholesterol 10 mg

Radicchio and fennel salad with oranges

Serves **4**   Preparation **25 minutes**

1 large head treviso radicchio
2 large oranges
1 large or 2 small fennel bulbs (about 1 kg/2 lb total) with leafy fronds
2 small white onions
4 tablespoons olive oil
1 tablespoon white wine vinegar
1 tablespoon lemon juice
1 sprig rosemary, leaves finely chopped
salt and freshly ground black pepper
1 cup (120 g/4 oz) pitted black olives

1 Line individual plates with radicchio leaves. Peel and segment oranges.

2 Using a vegetable peeler, slice fennel bulb into thin strips. Slice onions into thin rings.

3 Whisk oil, vinegar, lemon juice and rosemary in a bowl until combined. Season with salt and pepper to taste.

4 Finely chop a few fennel fronds. Layer fennel, oranges and onions onto radicchio. Drizzle with vinaigrette. Top with fennel fronds and olives.

PER SERVING kilojoules 1141, protein 4 g, total fat 19 g, saturated fat 3 g, carbohydrate 22 g, fibre 7 g, cholesterol 0 mg

Pasta, rice and grain salads

Pasta salad with peas and ham

Serves 4   Preparation 1 hour including chilling   Cooking 15 minutes

300 g (10 oz) fusilli (spiral pasta)
2 cups (240 g/8 oz) frozen peas
300 g (10 oz) ham, in one piece
10 small gherkins in vinegar, finely diced
3 medium tomatoes, halved and sliced
few sprigs of parsley

YOGURT MAYONNAISE
½ cup (125 g/4 oz) yogurt
½ cup (125 ml/4 fl oz) light mayonnaise
2 tablespoons white wine vinegar
salt and freshly ground black pepper
½ cup (40 g/2 oz) chopped fresh parsley

1 Cook pasta in plenty of lightly salted boiling water until al dente, following package instructions. Drain, rinse under cold running water and leave to cool. Cook peas in lightly salted water 2 to 3 minutes; leave to cool in cooking water.

2 Strain peas, reserving cooking water. Cut ham into small cubes. Combine pasta, peas, ham and gherkins in a serving bowl; mix well.

3 To make yogurt mayonnaise, whisk yogurt, mayonnaise, 4 tablespoons reserved cooking water and vinegar in a bowl until creamy and well combined. Season generously with salt and pepper. Stir in chopped parsley.

4 Stir dressing into salad. Chill, covered, 30 minutes. Garnish with tomatoes and parsley sprigs.

PER SERVING kilojoules 2053, protein 27 g, total fat 15 g, saturated fat 3 g, carbohydrate 61 g, fibre 9 g, cholesterol 54 mg

Asparagus and pasta

Serves 4   Preparation 15 minutes   Cooking 15 minutes

300 g (10 oz) fettuccine
500 g (1 lb) total of medium to thick green and white asparagus
2 tablespoons olive oil
1 tablespoon lemon-flavoured olive oil
2 tablespoons balsamic vinegar
salt and freshly ground black pepper
150 g (5 oz) fresh ricotta
3 to 4 tablespoons milk
1 tablespoon lemon juice
4 tablespoons freshly grated Parmesan
100 g (4 oz) Parma ham or other prosciutto
fresh basil leaves, for garnish

1 Cook pasta in plenty of lightly salted boiling water until al dente, following package instructions. Drain, rinse under cold running water and leave to cool. Trim ends from asparagus spears. Peel white asparagus from the tips to the ends and green asparagus only at the ends.

2 Using a sharp knife or vegetable peeler, slice asparagus lengthwise into thin strips. Place in a steamer basket. Fill a large saucepan with water to a depth equal to the width of two fingers; bring to a boil. Reduce heat to a simmer. Place steamer basket on top of pan. Cover; cook asparagus about 5 minutes or until crisp-tender. Drain, reserving cooking water. Leave to cool.

3 Whisk olive oil, lemon-flavoured olive oil, vinegar and 4 to 5 tablespoons reserved cooking water in a large bowl until combined. Add salt and pepper to taste. Add pasta; stir to coat with dressing. Stir in asparagus.

4 Combine ricotta, milk and lemon juice. Stir in Parmesan; add salt and pepper to taste. Trim fat from ham and cut ham into narrow strips. Arrange salad in individual bowls. Spoon a little ricotta mixture on each serving. Add ham. Garnish with basil leaves.

PER SERVING kilojoules 1976, protein 21 g, total fat 23 g, saturated fat 7 g, carbohydrate 45 g, fibre 4 g, cholesterol 39 mg

Farfalle salad with chicken

Serves **4** Preparation **20 minutes** Cooking **20 minutes**

250 g (8 oz) farfalle (bow-tie pasta)
4 medium zucchini (courgettes) (about 400 g/14 oz)
1 sprig fresh rosemary
1 clove garlic, finely chopped
3 tablespoons olive oil
salt and freshly ground black pepper
175 g (6 oz) rocket (arugula)
175 g (6 oz) cherry tomatoes, cut in half
3 tablespoons balsamic vinegar
3 sprigs each of fresh marjoram, thyme and flat-leaf parsley
2 tablespoons vegetable oil
400 g (14 oz) skinless chicken breast fillets, sliced into thin, even strips
1 tablespoon lemon juice

1 Cook pasta in plenty of lightly salted boiling water until al dente, following package instructions. Drain, rinse under cold running water and leave to cool. Cut zucchini into rounds. Roughly chop rosemary leaves. Combine zucchini, rosemary, garlic and 2 tablespoons olive oil in a bowl and leave for a few minutes.

2 Heat a nonstick pan over medium heat. Add zucchini mixture and cook until zucchini are golden brown. Sprinkle with salt and pepper and transfer to a large bowl with the pasta. Add rocket and tomatoes. Stir gently to combine.

3 Whisk vinegar, remaining 1 tablespoon olive oil, salt and pepper in a bowl until combined. Stir into salad.

4 Finely chop leaves of all the herbs. Heat vegetable oil in a nonstick pan over high heat and stir-fry chicken until golden brown. Season with salt and pepper.

5 Distribute pasta salad among serving bowls. Top with chicken and herbs and drizzle with lemon juice.

PER SERVING kilojoules 2399, protein 39 g, total fat 28 g, saturated fat 4 g, carbohydrate 39 g, fibre 6 g, cholesterol 85 mg

Green pasta salad

500 g (1 lb) green fettuccine
250 g (8 oz) cherry tomatoes
2 small Lebanese (Mediterranean) or pickling cucumbers
250 g (8 oz) rocket (arugula)
1 medium red onion, finely sliced
250 g (8 oz) bocconcini (baby mozzarella balls)
black olives for garnish

BASIL PESTO
1 cup (60 g/2 oz) fresh basil leaves
2 cloves garlic, roughly chopped
1 tablespoon pine nuts
4 tablespoons grated pecorino
6 tablespoons olive oil
3 tablespoons lemon juice
2 tablespoons vegetable stock (broth)
salt and freshly ground black pepper

1 Cook pasta in plenty of lightly salted boiling water until al dente, following package instructions. Drain, rinse under cold running water and leave to cool. Cut tomatoes in half. Slice cucumbers in half lengthwise and slice thinly.

2 Combine tomatoes, cucumbers, rocket, onion and pasta in a large bowl. Drain bocconcini and mix into the salad.

3 To make basil pesto, clean leaves by wiping them with paper towels; do not wash. Combine basil, garlic, pine nuts and pecorino in a food processor and process finely. Combine oil, lemon juice and stock in a small bowl and add to mixture in a steady stream with the motor running until amalgamated. Add salt and pepper to taste.

4 Stir basil pesto into salad or serve separately. Spoon salad into individual bowls and garnish with olives.

PER SERVING kilojoules 2296, protein 19 g, total fat 29 g, saturated fat 8 g, carbohydrate 52 g, fibre 6 g, cholesterol 20 mg

Farfalle salad with beans and ham

Serves 4   Preparation 40 minutes including cooling   Cooking 10 minutes

300 g (10 oz) farfalle (bow-tie pasta)
400 g (14 oz) fresh butter (yellow wax) beans, trimmed
6 sprigs thyme
½ teaspoon salt
250 g (8 oz) ham, in one piece
2 shallots, finely diced
4 large red radishes, cut into quarters, for garnish

PAPRIKA SOUR CREAM DRESSING
200 g (7 oz) light sour cream
1 tablespoon vegetable oil
2 tablespoons herb vinegar
salt and freshly ground black pepper
¼ teaspoon ground sweet paprika

1 Cook pasta in plenty of lightly salted boiling water until al dente, following package instructions. Drain, rinse under cold running water and leave to cool.

2 Place beans, 3 sprigs thyme and ½ teaspoon salt in a saucepan and cover with water. Cook, covered, 10 minutes or until crisp-tender. Drain, reserving cooking water. Briefly immerse in iced water and drain again.

3 Trim ham of excess fat and cut into narrow strips. Combine pasta, beans, shallots and ham in a large bowl. Finely chop leaves from remaining 3 sprigs thyme.

4 To make dressing, mix sour cream, 2 tablespoons cooking water, oil, vinegar, salt, pepper, sweet paprika and chopped thyme in a bowl until creamy.

5 Stir dressing into salad. Divide salad among four bowls and garnish with radishes.

PER SERVING kilojoules 1867, protein 22 g, total fat 18 g, saturated fat 8 g, carbohydrate 47 g, fibre 6 g, cholesterol 62 mg

Orecchiette salad with tuna and aïoli

Serves **4** Preparation **20 minutes** Cooking **8 minutes**

350 g (12 oz) orecchiette (little ears pasta)
250 g (8 oz) green asparagus
1 medium zucchini (courgette)
1 medium orange capsicum (bell pepper)
1 can (180 g/7 oz) tuna in water, drained
1 cup (120 g/4 oz) pitted green olives

HERB VINAIGRETTE
2 tablespoons red wine vinegar
2 tablespoons sunflower oil
salt and freshly ground black pepper
1 teaspoon dried mixed herbs

AÏOLI
2 cloves garlic
½ teaspoon salt
1 egg yolk
1 tablespoon white wine vinegar
½ cup (125 ml/4 fl oz) olive oil
1 tablespoon lemon juice
salt and freshly ground black pepper

1 Cook pasta in plenty of lightly salted boiling water until al dente, following package instructions. Drain, rinse under cold running water and leave to cool. Trim asparagus and cut into small pieces. Place in a steamer basket. Fill a large saucepan with water to a depth equal to the width of two fingers; bring to a boil. Reduce heat to a simmer. Place steamer basket on top of pan. Cover and cook asparagus 6 to 8 minutes. Leave to cool.

2 Slice zucchini into rounds. Cut capsicum in half and chop into small pieces. Separate tuna into flakes with a fork. Finely chop olives.

3 To make herb vinaigrette, whisk all the ingredients in a large bowl until combined. Add pasta, asparagus, zucchini, capsicum and olives.

4 To make aïoli, have all ingredients at room temperature to avoid curdling. Grind garlic and ½ teaspoon salt to a fine paste in a bowl. Using electric beaters or a whisk, beat in egg yolk and ½ tablespoon vinegar until creamy. Add oil, drop by drop at first, then in a steady stream. Beat until mixture is thick and creamy. Season well with remaining ½ tablespoon vinegar, lemon juice and salt and pepper to taste.

5 Distribute salad among serving bowls and add tuna. Spoon a little aïoli on top.

PER SERVING kilojoules 2293, protein 19 g, total fat 26 g, saturated fat 4 g, carbohydrate 58 g, fibre 5 g, cholesterol 41 mg

Noodle and mushroom sweet and sour salad

Serves **4**   Preparation **30 minutes including soaking**   Cooking **10 minutes**

250 g (8 oz) glass (cellophane) noodles
250 g (8 oz) fresh shiitake mushrooms
250 g (8 oz) Chinese (napa) cabbage
2 medium carrots (about 250 g/8 oz)
3 tablespoons vegetable oil
1 clove garlic, finely chopped
1 tablespoon finely chopped fresh ginger root
2 tablespoons soy sauce
2 tablespoons rice vinegar
2 teaspoons soft brown sugar
1 tablespoon lime juice
salt and freshly ground black pepper
2 red chilies, finely sliced

1 Pour boiling water over noodles; leave 10 minutes. Wipe mushrooms with paper towels, remove stalks and slice large caps in half, leaving others whole.

2 Slice cabbage into quarters and remove core. Slice cabbage thinly. Cut carrots into fine strips. Drain noodles and cut into short lengths.

3 Combine noodles, cabbage and carrots in a bowl. Heat oil in a pan and sauté mushrooms over high heat. Add garlic and ginger and cook another 3 minutes. Stir in soy sauce and 1 tablespoon rice vinegar. Remove from heat. Add brown sugar, lime juice and salt and pepper to taste. Leave to cool.

4 Combine mushroom mixture and noodle mixture. Add remaining 1 tablespoon rice vinegar and season to taste with salt and pepper. Distribute among individual serving dishes. Sprinkle with chilies.

PER SERVING kilojoules 1377, protein 3 g, total fat 14 g, saturated fat 2 g, carbohydrate 45 g, fibre 6 g, cholesterol 0 mg

Salami rice salad

Serves 4   Preparation 30 minutes including cooling   Cooking 35 minutes

¾ cup (140 g/5 oz) long-grain rice
350 ml (12 fl oz) salt-reduced vegetable stock (broth)
500 g (1 lb) broccoli
1 medium yellow capsicum (bell pepper)
175 g (6 oz) spicy salami, in one piece
leaves of 3 sprigs thyme, finely chopped
½ teaspoon ground sweet paprika

DRESSING
3 tablespoons light mayonnaise
½ cup (125 g/4 oz) yogurt
1 tablespoon olive oil
2 tablespoons white wine vinegar
herb salt
freshly ground black pepper

1 Place rice and stock in a saucepan, cover and bring to a boil. Reduce heat to low, half cover pan and cook rice 15 to 20 minutes or until cooked. Remove from heat. Let stand, uncovered, until cool, loosening rice occasionally with a fork.

2 Chop broccoli into small pieces. Place in a steamer basket. Fill a large saucepan with water to a depth equal to the width of two fingers; bring to a boil. Reduce heat to a simmer. Place steamer basket on top of pan. Cover; cook broccoli 8 to 12 minutes, or until crisp-tender. Remove from steamer and leave to cool. Reserve cooking liquid.

3 Halve capsicum and cut into small strips. Peel salami and cut into small strips.

4 To make dressing, whisk mayonnaise, yogurt, oil and 1 tablespoon vinegar in a large bowl until well combined. Add herb salt and pepper to taste. Add rice, vegetables and salami and stir to combine. If salad is too dry, mix in 3 to 4 tablespoons of reserved cooking liquid.

5 Mix half the thyme into the salad. Check seasoning, adding remaining 1 tablespoon vinegar and salt and pepper to taste. Sprinkle with paprika and remaining thyme.

PER SERVING kilojoules 1896, protein 20 g, total fat 25 g, saturated fat 8 g, carbohydrate 37 g, fibre 5 g, cholesterol 34 mg

Spicy brown rice salad with feta

Serves 4   Preparation 30 minutes (plus soaking overnight)   Cooking 1 hour

1 cup (200 g/7 oz) brown rice
½ teaspoon salt
300 g (10 oz) mini (Japanese) or large eggplants (aubergines)
4 tablespoons olive oil
1 clove garlic, finely sliced
2 tablespoons ajvar (spicy capsicum and eggplant relish)
3 tablespoons lemon juice
½ to 1 teaspoon dried chili flakes
finely chopped leaves of 4 sprigs mint
salt and freshly ground black pepper
3 large tomatoes, diced
heart of 1 cos (romaine) lettuce
125 g (4 oz) feta cheese, cubed
⅔ cup (100 g/4 oz) kalamata olives

1 Mix rice, 2 cups (500 ml/16 fl oz) water and ½ teaspoon salt in a saucepan. Cover and soak overnight. Bring rice to a boil, uncovered. Cook half covered over low heat for 40 minutes. Remove from heat; leave to cool. Loosen rice occasionally with a fork.

2 Leave mini eggplants whole. Dice large ones. Heat 3 tablespoons oil in a nonstick pan over medium heat. Cook eggplants about 10 minutes, turning occasionally.

3 Add garlic and cook 2 minutes. Remove pan from heat, leave to cool.

4 Combine ajvar, 2 tablespoons lemon juice, remaining 2 tablespoons oil, chili flakes and mint in a large bowl; season with salt and pepper to taste. Mix in cooked rice and tomatoes. Season with remaining 1 tablespoon lemon juice and salt and pepper to taste.

5 Line a serving plate with lettuce. Top with salad, eggplants, feta and olives.

PER SERVING kilojoules 2393, protein 15 g, total fat 29 g, saturated fat 8 g, carbohydrate 64 g, fibre 8 g, cholesterol 22 mg

Rice salad with ginger-soy dressing

Serves 4   Preparation 1 hour including cooling   Cooking 20 to 25 minutes

¾ cup (140 g/5 oz) basmati or other fragrant rice
½ teaspoon salt
125 g (4 oz) fresh baby corn (about 10)
150 g (5 oz) snow peas (mange-tout)
1 medium red capsicum (bell pepper)
3 spring onions (scallions), finely chopped
1 can (190 g/7 oz) bamboo shoots, drained
4 tablespoons roasted cashew nuts

GINGER-SOY DRESSING
1 tablespoon finely grated fresh ginger root
3 tablespoons rice vinegar
2 tablespoons soy sauce
2 tablespoons sunflower or peanut oil
1 tablespoon medium–hot mango chutney

1 Combine rice, 1 cup (250 ml/8 fl oz) water and salt in a saucepan and bring to a boil. Half cover rice and cook over low heat 20 to 25 minutes. Remove from heat. Leave to cool. Loosen rice occasionally with a fork.

2 Bring a pan of lightly salted water to a boil. Blanch corn 3 minutes and snow peas 1 minute. Drain, immerse in iced water to arrest cooking. Drain; leave to cool.

3 Halve capsicum and cut into narrow strips. Cut snow peas and corn in half. Mix rice and all the salad vegetables in a large bowl.

4 To make ginger-soy dressing, combine vinegar, soy sauce, oil and chutney in a bowl. (If chutney contains large pieces of mango, break them up with a fork before adding.) Stir to combine.

5 Stir dressing into rice salad. Arrange salad on serving plates and sprinkle with cashew nuts.

PER SERVING kilojoules 1386, protein 8 g, total fat 16 g, saturated fat 2 g, carbohydrate 39 g, fibre 4 g, cholesterol 0 mg

Spicy rice salad with pineapple

Serves 4   Preparation 40 minutes including cooling   Cooking 25 minutes

1 cup (185 g/7 oz) basmati rice
½ teaspoon salt
1 cup (200 g/7 oz) drained canned pineapple slices or pieces in natural juice
4 stalks celery
300 g (10 oz) small mushrooms, chopped
2 spring onions (scallions), sliced
4 to 6 large Chinese (napa) cabbage leaves

CURRY VINAIGRETTE
100 g (4 oz) crème fraîche or light sour cream
3 tablespoons milk
2 tablespoons raspberry vinegar
1 tablespoon sunflower oil
¼ teaspoon ground ginger
1 teaspoon mild curry powder
¼ to ½ teaspoon sambal oelek or Chinese chili paste

1 Place rice in a saucepan with 400 ml (14 fl oz) water and ½ teaspoon salt. Bring to a boil, uncovered. Cover pan and cook rice over low heat 15 to 20 minutes or until all liquid is absorbed. Rice should be light and fluffy with steam holes on the surface. Turn off heat, let stand, covered, another 5 minutes. Remove from heat, uncover pan and let rice cool. Loosen grains occasionally with a fork.

2 Chop pineapple slices into small pieces. Slice celery into thin strips. Reserve feathery leaves. Combine rice, pineapple, celery and mushrooms in a large bowl. Add spring onions, reserving a few for garnish.

3 To make dressing, whisk crème fraîche, milk, vinegar, oil, ginger, curry and ¼ teaspoon sambal oelek in a bowl until creamy. Add remaining ¼ teaspoon sambal oelek to taste. Stir into salad ingredients.

4 Cut Chinese cabbage leaves into strips. Divide among individual serving plates and top with rice salad. Garnish with celery leaves and reserved spring onion rings.

PER SERVING kilojoules 1551, protein 8 g, total fat 16 g, saturated fat 8 g, carbohydrate 47 g, fibre 6 g, cholesterol 33 mg

Potato and lentil salad

Serves 6   Preparation 15 minutes   Cooking 20 minutes

1 kg (2 lb) waxy potatoes, peeled and cut into large chunks
½ cup (125 ml/4 fl oz) olive oil
2 tablespoons red wine vinegar
4 cups (750 g/1 lb 10 oz) cooked brown lentils
1 cup (120 g/4 oz) pitted black olives
1 tablespoon capers, chopped
2 cloves garlic, chopped
1 tablespoon lemon juice
⅔ cup (55 g/2 oz) roughly chopped fresh flat-leaf parsley
6 spring onions (scallions), sliced diagonally
freshly ground black pepper

1 Cook potatoes in a pan of boiling water 20 minutes or until tender. Drain and transfer to a large bowl.

2 While potatoes are still hot, whisk oil and vinegar and stir in. Carefully mix in lentils, olives, capers, garlic, lemon juice, parsley, spring onions and a good grinding of pepper. Serve while still warm.

PER SERVING kilojoules 1553, protein 13 g, total fat 20 g, saturated fat 3 g, carbohydrate 36 g, fibre 9 g, cholesterol 0 mg

Lentil salad with fried onions and rosemary

Serves 4   Preparation 1 hour 35 minutes including chilling
Cooking 40 minutes to 1 hour

2 cups (400 g/14 oz) Puy-style green lentils
1 small sprig rosemary
1 small dried bay leaf
3 small unpeeled cooked potatoes
2 large tomatoes, cored and diced
2 tablespoons olive oil
2 tablespoons red wine or herb vinegar
1 tablespoon lemon juice
1 teaspoon grated lemon peel
½ teaspoon ground cumin
1 clove garlic, crushed
salt and freshly ground black pepper
2 large white onions, sliced into rings
2 tablespoons olive oil
½ cup (40 g/2 oz) finely chopped fresh flat-leaf parsley

1   Place lentils, rosemary and bay leaf in a saucepan. Add water to cover; bring to a boil. Cook on medium heat about 40 minutes or until soft. Leave to cool in cooking liquid. Drain, reserving liquid. Discard rosemary and bay leaf.

2   Peel and dice potatoes and place in a large bowl with tomatoes and lentils. Whisk oil, vinegar, lemon juice, peel, cumin, garlic and 3 tablespoons reserved cooking liquid in a small bowl. Add salt and pepper to taste. Stir into salad. Chill salad, covered, 1 hour.

3   Cook onion rings in oil over moderate heat until golden brown. Check salad for seasoning, adding more salt, pepper and vinegar, if needed. Stir in parsley.

4   Distribute salad among individual serving bowls and top with warm onions.

PER SERVING kilojoules 1573, protein 17 g, total fat 19 g, saturated fat 3 g, carbohydrate 34 g, fibre 11 g, cholesterol 0 mg

White bean salad with sesame dressing

Serves 4   Preparation 25 minutes plus 12 hours soaking   Cooking 45 minutes

1 cup (200 g/7 oz) dried small white beans
2 medium tomatoes, cored and diced
1 medium red onion, thinly sliced
2 mild light green banana chilies (capsicums), cut in thin strips
3 tablespoons olive oil
3 tablespoons red wine vinegar
salt and freshly ground black pepper
4 tablespoons tahini (sesame paste)
2 tablespoons lemon juice
2 medium eggs, hard-boiled, sliced
⅓ cup (50 g/2 oz) black olives
½ cup (40 g/2 oz) fresh parsley leaves

1 Soak beans in water overnight. Drain. Place in a pan and cover with water. Bring to a boil; cook 35 minutes or until soft. Let cool in cooking water. Drain.

2 Place beans in a serving bowl. Add tomatoes, onion and chilies. Whisk oil, vinegar, salt and pepper and stir into salad.

3 Combine tahini, lemon juice and about 4 tablespoons water in a bowl; stir until smooth. Add salt to taste. Add eggs, olives and parsley to salad. Spoon on sesame dressing.

PER SERVING kilojoules 1847, protein 19 g, total fat 30 g, saturated fat 5 g, carbohydrate 23 g, fibre 16 g, cholesterol 108 mg

Buckwheat and artichoke salad with feta

Serves **4**   Preparation **1 hour 30 minutes including cooling**   Cooking **20 minutes**

2 cups (500 ml/16 fl oz) salt-reduced vegetable stock (broth)
1 bay leaf
1 cup (180 g/7 oz) wholegrain roasted buckwheat groats (kasha)
2 teaspoons olive oil
1 can (280 g/10 oz) artichoke hearts, drained
1 medium head round radicchio
2 large tomatoes
1 sprig rosemary
4 sprigs marjoram
2 tablespoons olive oil
1 tablespoon balsamic vinegar
3 tablespoons lemon juice
salt and freshly ground black pepper
150 g (5 oz) feta cheese, cubed

1 Place stock, bay leaf and buckwheat in a saucepan and bring to a boil, uncovered. Add oil. Reduce heat to very low. Cover pan; simmer 15 minutes. Remove from heat and leave, covered, 10 minutes. Uncover; fluff buckwheat with a fork. Season with salt to taste. Let cool.

2 Chop artichoke hearts into small pieces. Tear radicchio into small pieces. Halve and core tomatoes, remove seeds. Cut flesh into small cubes.

3 Finely chop rosemary and marjoram leaves. Whisk herbs, oil, vinegar and 2 tablespoons lemon juice in a large serving bowl. Add salt and pepper to taste. Add buckwheat, artichokes, radicchio and tomatoes; stir to combine.

4 Leave salad, covered, 1 hour. Just before serving, add salt, pepper and remaining lemon juice to taste. Add feta and stir to combine.

PER SERVING kilojoules 1781, protein 14 g, total fat 25 g, saturated fat 8 g, carbohydrate 35 g, fibre 4 g, cholesterol 26 mg

Couscous salad with chickpeas

Serves 4   Preparation 35 minutes including standing

1⅓ cups (240 g/8 oz) instant couscous
½ teaspoon salt
4 roma (plum) tomatoes
2 spring onions (scallions)
½ cup (40 g/2 oz) finely chopped fresh flat-leaf parsley
1 can (300 g/10 oz) chickpeas (garbanzo beans), rinsed and drained
200 g (7 oz) garlic sausage or cabanossi, in one piece

VINAIGRETTE
3 tablespoons olive oil
1 tablespoon red wine vinegar
2 tablespoons lemon juice
1 clove garlic, crushed
1 teaspoon ground cumin
1 teaspoon ground sweet paprika
salt and freshly ground black pepper

1 Bring 1 cup (250 ml/8 fl oz) water to a boil in a medium saucepan. Remove from heat. Stir in couscous and salt and leave to absorb liquid 20 minutes. Leave to cool.

2 Halve and core tomatoes and cut into small dice. Slice spring onions into rings.

3 To make vinaigrette, whisk oil, vinegar, 2 tablespoons lemon juice, garlic, cumin and paprika in a large bowl. Add salt and pepper to taste. Stir parsley, couscous, chickpeas, tomatoes and spring onions into vinaigrette.

4 Just before serving, taste salad and season with salt, pepper and remaining 1 tablespoon lemon juice. Slice sausage into small cubes and stir in.

PER SERVING kilojoules 1591, protein 13 g, total fat 27 g, saturated fat 7 g, carbohydrate 20 g, fibre 4 g, cholesterol 22 mg

Chickpea, spinach and eggplant salad

Serves **4**   Preparation **5 minutes**   Cooking **6 minutes**

2 medium eggplants (aubergines) (about 500 g/1 lb in total), thinly sliced
¼ cup (60 ml/2 fl oz) olive oil
150 g (5 oz) baby spinach leaves
1 cup (175 g/6 oz) cooked chickpeas
150 g (5 oz) feta cheese, crumbled
1 small red onion, thinly sliced
3 tablespoons chopped fresh mint leaves
2 tablespoons lemon juice

1 Brush eggplant slices with half the oil. Place in a large nonstick pan over medium–high heat. Cook 2 to 3 minutes each side until golden.

2 Place spinach on a serving platter and top with eggplant, chickpeas, feta, onion and mint.

3 Combine remaining oil and lemon juice. Pour over salad and serve.

PER SERVING kilojoules 1325, protein 12 g, total fat 25 g, saturated fat 8 g, carbohydrate 12 g, fibre 6 g, cholesterol 26 mg

MEXICAN BEEF SALAD

HAM AND CHEESE SALAD

PASTRAMI AND ARTICHOKE SALAD

VEAL AND MUSHROOM SALAD WITH BASIL

SPICY PORK SALAD

MIXED SALAD WITH HAM

CHICKEN WITH MIXED SALAD GREENS

Meat and poultry salads

TARRAGON CHICKEN SALAD

CHICKEN SALAD WITH CUCUMBER
AND WATERCRESS

CHICKEN AND PINEAPPLE SALAD
WITH CURRY DRESSING

CHICKEN KEBAB SALAD

CHICKEN LIVER AND APPLE SALAD

TURKEY AND MUSHROOM SALAD

Mexican beef salad

Serves **4**   Preparation **1 hour 35 minutes including marinating**

500 g (1 lb) cooked lean beef
2 long red chilies
½ cup (30 g/1 oz) finely chopped fresh coriander (cilantro) leaves
4 tablespoons olive oil
3 tablespoons red wine vinegar
2 tablespoons lime juice
¼ teaspoon sweet ground paprika
salt and freshly ground black pepper
1 red capsicum (bell pepper)
1 orange capsicum (bell pepper)
8 drained and rinsed canned baby corn spears
2 large tomatoes
2 spring onions (scallions), thinly sliced
50 g (2 oz) corn chips

1 Cut beef into narrow strips; place in a bowl. Chop chilies finely; discard seeds. Add to bowl. Add coriander, reserving 1 tablespoon for garnish.

2 To make vinaigrette, whisk oil, 2 tablespoons vinegar, lime juice and paprika in a bowl. Add salt and pepper to taste. Stir into beef mixture. Chill, covered, 1 hour.

3 Dice capsicums. Cut baby corn spears in half. Halve tomatoes, remove core and seeds; dice. Add to beef mixture with spring onions and remaining 1 tablespoon vinegar.

4 Just before serving, add salt and pepper to taste. Divide salad among serving bowls. Add corn chips and sprinkle with reserved coriander.

PER SERVING kilojoules 2039, protein 40 g, total fat 30 g, saturated fat 8 g, carbohydrate 12 g, fibre 4 g, cholesterol 88 mg

Ham and cheese salad

Serves 4   Preparation 1 hour 20 minutes including marinating

400 g (14 oz) ham
250 g (8 oz) reduced-fat Swiss-style cheese, thinly sliced
150 g (5 oz) small gherkins in vinegar
2 medium red onions
½ cup (30 g/1 oz) finely chopped chives

VINAIGRETTE
2 tablespoons vegetable oil
3 to 4 tablespoons white wine vinegar
4 tablespoons gherkin liquid
4 tablespoons beef stock (broth)
1 teaspoon hot mustard
salt and freshly ground black pepper

1 Cut ham into fine strips. Cut cheese and gherkins into fine strips. Finely dice onions. Combine ham, cheese, gherkins and onions in a large bowl.

2 To make vinaigrette, whisk oil, vinegar, 2 tablespoons gherkin liquid, stock and mustard in a bowl. Add salt and pepper to taste.

3 Pour vinaigrette over salad and toss to combine. Chill, covered, 1 hour. Add remaining 2 tablespoons gherkin liquid and salt and pepper to taste. Sprinkle with chives.

PER SERVING kilojoules 1507, protein 33 g, total fat 23 g, saturated fat 8 g, carbohydrate 4 g, fibre 1 g, cholesterol 78 mg

Pastrami and artichoke salad

Serves 4   Preparation 1 hour 35 minutes including chilling

300 g (10 oz) thinly sliced pastrami
4 tablespoons olive oil
1 tablespoon balsamic vinegar
2 tablespoons lemon juice
salt and freshly ground black pepper
100 g (4 oz) rocket (arugula)
6 marinated artichoke hearts, drained
3 ripe roma (plum) tomatoes, sliced
1 medium red onion, thinly sliced into rings

1 Place pastrami on a plate. To make vinaigrette, whisk oil, vinegar and lemon juice in a bowl. Add salt and pepper to taste. Drizzle half the vinaigrette over pastrami. Chill, covered, 1 hour.

2 Line serving plates with rocket. Cut artichoke hearts into quarters and arrange on plates with tomatoes. Add pastrami and top with onion rings. Drizzle with remaining vinaigrette.

PER SERVING kilojoules 1275, protein 19 g, total fat 23 g, saturated fat 5 g, carbohydrate 4 g, fibre 3 g, cholesterol 51 mg

Veal and mushroom salad with basil

Serves **4**   Preparation **15 minutes**   Cooking **15 minutes**

500 g (1 lb) veal or chicken schnitzels, cut thin
5 tablespoons olive oil
1 clove garlic, finely chopped
3 spring onions (scallions), finely sliced
500 g (1 lb) mixed small mushrooms, such as button,
    Swiss brown (cremini) or shiitake, sliced
salt and freshly ground black pepper
1 cup (60 g/2 oz) basil leaves
45 g (1½ oz) Parmesan, in one piece
4 tablespoons beef stock (broth)
2 tablespoons port wine
2 tablespoons balsamic vinegar
150 g (5 oz) cherry tomatoes, cut in half

1 Cut veal into thin, even strips. Heat 3 tablespoons oil in a nonstick pan over high heat. Sear veal briefly both sides. Add garlic and spring onions; cook 1 minute. Transfer to a plate and keep warm.

2 Heat remaining 2 tablespoons oil in pan. Fry mushrooms over medium heat 5 minutes. Add salt and pepper to taste. Transfer to a plate. Slice basil finely; keep a few leaves whole for garnish. Use a vegetable peeler to shave Parmesan into thin slices.

3 Place stock and port in pan in which veal was cooked; bring to a boil and cook briefly over high heat, stirring in juices and any crusty pieces from the meat. Transfer to a bowl. Add vinegar and salt and pepper to taste. When completely cooled, mix in two thirds of chopped basil.

4 Combine veal and mushrooms; place on a serving plate. Drizzle on stock mixture. Top with Parmesan. Garnish with remaining chopped basil, whole basil leaves and tomatoes.

PER SERVING kilojoules 1860, protein 35 g, total fat 30 g, saturated fat 7 g, carbohydrate 5 g, fibre 4 g, cholesterol 104 mg

Spicy pork salad

Serves 4   Preparation 30 minutes

500 g (1 lb) cooked lean pork
250 g (8 oz) Chinese (napa) cabbage
1 can (190 g/7 oz) bamboo shoots, drained
100 g (4 oz) snow peas (mange-tout)
1 small piece fresh ginger root
1 tablespoon chopped lemongrass
2 tablespoons vegetable oil
½ teaspoon sesame oil
3 tablespoons rice vinegar
2 tablespoons salt-reduced soy sauce
1 teaspoon soft brown sugar
salt, to taste
2 tablespoons sesame seeds
2 tablespoons sour cream
1 teaspoon sambal oelek or Chinese chili paste
3 tablespoons finely chopped chives

1 Cut pork into very thin strips and place in a bowl. Finely shred Chinese cabbage. Cut bamboo shoots into thin strips. Cut snow peas into strips. Add all vegetables to bowl.

2 Finely chop ginger. Finely chop lemongrass: first remove hard outer layers and cut off the root, trim off woody ends from leaves, then cut the tender leaves crosswise into strips.

3 To make vinaigrette, whisk vegetable oil, sesame oil, 2 tablespoons rice vinegar, soy sauce and sugar in a bowl. Add ginger and lemongrass; whisk to combine. Check seasoning, adding salt to taste. Stir vinaigrette into salad.

4 Toast sesame seeds in a frying pan over medium heat until golden, stirring occasionally. Transfer to a plate and set aside to cool. Combine sour cream and sambal oelek.

5 Taste salad, adding salt and remaining 1 tablespoon rice vinegar, if necessary. Spoon salad onto serving plates. Top with a little sour cream mixture. Sprinkle with sesame seeds and chives.

PER SERVING kilojoules 1711, protein 39 g, total fat 25 g, saturated fat 7 g, carbohydrate 6 g, fibre 4 g, cholesterol 128 mg

Mixed salad with ham

Serves 4   Preparation 25 minutes   Cooking 5 minutes

250 g (8 oz) smoked ham
1⅔ cups (200 g/7 oz) frozen peas
salt
2 medium carrots (about 250 g/8 oz)
2 small cucumbers
½ cup (100 g/4 oz) drained pickled onions
2 large tomatoes, cored and diced
100 g (4 oz) lamb's lettuce (corn salad/mâche)
alfalfa or mung bean sprouts or mustard cress, for garnish

CREAMY DRESSING
3 tablespoons mayonnaise
⅔ cup (170 g/6 oz) Greek-style yogurt
1 teaspoon Dijon mustard
2 tablespoons lemon juice
pinch of sugar
salt and freshly ground black pepper

1 Trim excess fat from ham; cut ham into small cubes. Cook peas in lightly salted boiling water for 5 minutes. Drain, reserving cooking liquid. Leave peas to cool.

2 Coarsely grate carrots. Quarter cucumbers lengthwise, scoop out seeds with a small spoon and cut flesh into small pieces. Cut pickled onions in half. Place carrots, cucumbers, pickled onions, tomatoes and peas in a bowl.

3 To make creamy dressing, whisk mayonnaise, yogurt, mustard, lemon juice, sugar and 3 tablespoons reserved cooking liquid in a bowl. Add salt and pepper to taste.

4 Stir dressing into salad. Distribute among serving bowls. Add lamb's lettuce and alfalfa sprouts.

PER SERVING kilojoules 1151, protein 19 g, total fat 12 g, saturated fat 4 g, carbohydrate 22 g, fibre 7 g, cholesterol 49 mg

Chicken with mixed salad greens

Serves 4   Preparation 1 hour 15 minutes including chilling   Cooking 5 minutes

2 skinless chicken breast fillets (about 300 g/10 oz in total)
1 large clove garlic, crushed
1 head oak leaf lettuce
1 small head curly endive (frisée) lettuce
1 head treviso or round radicchio
2 tablespoons olive oil
salt and freshly ground black pepper
1 small lemon
3 spring onions (scallions), finely sliced
250 g (8 oz) button mushrooms, thinly sliced

DRESSING
½ cup (125 g/4 oz) light sour cream
½ cup (125 g/4 oz) low-fat yogurt
1 tablespoon vegetable oil
1 tablespoon white wine vinegar
1 teaspoon Dijon mustard
salt and freshly ground black pepper

1 Cut chicken into strips. Place chicken and garlic in a bowl. Stir to combine. Chill, covered, 1 hour. Cut or tear oak leaf lettuce, curly endive and radicchio into small pieces. Place in a large bowl.

2 Heat oil in a nonstick pan over medium heat. Cook chicken until golden brown and cooked through, about 5 minutes. Add salt and pepper to taste.

3 To make dressing, whisk sour cream, yogurt, oil, vinegar and mustard in a bowl until combined. Add salt and pepper to taste. Stir dressing into salad greens. Distribute salad greens among serving plates.

4 Peel thin strips of rind from lemon. Place chicken, spring onions, mushrooms and lemon rind on top of salad greens.

PER SERVING kilojoules 1491, protein 24 g, total fat 25 g, saturated fat 7 g, carbohydrate 10 g, fibre 5 g, cholesterol 71 mg

Tarragon chicken salad

Serves **4**   Preparation **20 minutes**   Cooking **20 minutes**

2 skinless chicken breast fillets (about 300 g/10 oz in total)
350 ml (12 fl oz) salt-reduced chicken or vegetable stock (broth)
2 long sprigs tarragon
1 small lemon
3 black peppercorns
2 tablespoons tahini (sesame paste)
salt and freshly ground black pepper
1 medium head witlof (Belgian endive/chicory)
150 g (5 oz) baby spinach leaves
2 large oranges, peeled and segmented
½ cup (45 g/2 oz) flaked almonds, toasted

1 Place chicken in a single layer in a shallow pan. Cover with stock. Remove leaves from tarragon sprigs; set aside. Lightly crush stalks with a rolling pin, then add to pan. Using a vegetable peeler, remove a wide strip of rind from lemon. Add to pan with peppercorns.

2 Place pan over moderate heat and bring stock to a boil. Reduce heat to a simmer, cover pan and cook 15 minutes, or until chicken is cooked through. Remove chicken from pan with a slotted spoon; leave to cool. Strain stock and reserve. Discard stalks, rind and peppercorns.

3 To make dressing, whisk tahini with 4 tablespoons reserved stock. Add another 1 to 2 tablespoons if mixture is too thick. Squeeze juice from lemon; stir into dressing. Chop enough tarragon leaves to make 1 tablespoon. Add to dressing. Add salt and pepper to taste.

4 Slice witlof diagonally into narrow pieces. Place on a large serving platter with spinach leaves. Add orange segments and toasted almonds. Slice chicken into wide strips and add to salad. Spoon on dressing.

PER SERVING kilojoules 1274, protein 30 g, total fat 15 g, saturated fat 2 g, carbohydrate 10 g, fibre 5 g, cholesterol 64 mg

Chicken salad with cucumber and watercress

Serves 4   Preparation 1 hour 15 minutes including chilling   Cooking 12 minutes

1 sprig rosemary
1 clove garlic, roughly chopped
2 skinless chicken breast fillets
  (about 300 g/10 oz in total)
2 tablespoons lime juice
salt and freshly ground black pepper
3 small Lebanese (Mediterranean)
  cucumbers
150 g (5 oz) watercress
3 tablespoons finely chopped fresh
  chervil
3 tablespoons finely chopped
  fresh dill
3 tablespoons finely chopped chives
2 tablespoons sunflower or peanut oil

MUSTARD AND LEMON DRESSING
½ cup (125 g/4 oz) light sour cream
½ cup (125 g/4 oz) yogurt
50 ml (2 fl oz) milk
½ teaspoon tarragon or other herb
  mustard
1 tablespoon olive oil
2 tablespoons lemon juice
salt and freshly ground black pepper

1 Roughly chop rosemary leaves and combine with garlic in a bowl. Add chicken; turn to coat. Drizzle with lime juice and sprinkle with salt and pepper. Chill, covered, 1 hour.

2 Peel fine strips of skin lengthwise from cucumber. Slice cucumbers thinly. Divide watercress into small sprigs.

3 To make mustard and lemon dressing, whisk sour cream, yogurt, milk, mustard, oil and lemon juice in a large bowl until combined. Add salt and pepper to taste. Add cucumber, watercress and herbs to bowl. Stir to coat completely with dressing.

4 Heat oil in a nonstick frying pan over medium heat. Add chicken and cook, turning occasionally, 8 to 10 minutes, until cooked through. Remove from pan and set aside for a few minutes.

5 Arrange cucumber and watercress salad on individual plates. Cut chicken crosswise into thick slices; add to salad.

PER SERVING kilojoules 1504, protein 28 g, total fat 24 g, saturated fat 7 g, carbohydrate 6 g, fibre 3 g, cholesterol 89 mg

Chicken and pineapple salad with curry dressing

Serves **4**   Preparation **30 minutes**   Cooking **1 hour 15 minutes**

1 ready-to-cook chicken (about
    1.6 kg/3 lb)
2 medium onions, roughly chopped
2 celery stalks, roughly chopped
2 medium carrots (about 250 g/8 oz),
    roughly chopped
1 bay leaf
2 teaspoons salt
1 teaspoon whole black peppercorns
½ small sweet pineapple (about
    500 g/1 lb)
3 mandarins, tangerines or small
    oranges
2 thin leeks
heart of 1 cos (romaine) lettuce
lemon balm leaves, for garnish

CURRY DRESSING
4 tablespoons light mayonnaise
½ cup (125 g/4 oz) yogurt
4 tablespoons orange juice
2 tablespoons lemon juice
2 teaspoons mild curry powder
pinch of ground ginger
pinch of cayenne pepper
salt and freshly ground black pepper

1 Place chicken, chopped vegetables, bay leaf, salt and peppercorns in a large saucepan. Cover with water. Bring to a boil. Skim off surface with a slotted spoon. Cook, partly covered, over low heat 1 hour 15 minutes. Remove pan from heat. Leave chicken to cool in cooking liquid.

2 Separate chicken meat from carcass and chop flesh into small pieces; place in a bowl. Trim pineapple, discard core and cut fruit into small pieces. Peel and segment 2 mandarins. Add pineapple and mandarin pieces to chicken. Cut leeks in half lengthwise and cut into very fine strips. Add to bowl.

3 To make curry dressing, whisk mayonnaise, yogurt, orange juice and lemon juice until combined. Stir in curry powder, ginger and cayenne pepper. Add salt and pepper to taste. Stir dressing into chicken and pineapple mixture.

4 Peel and slice remaining mandarin crosswise. Tear or cut lettuce into wide strips. Distribute among serving bowls and top with chicken salad. Garnish with mandarin slices and lemon balm leaves.

PER SERVING kilojoules 1729, protein 43 g, total fat 15 g, saturated fat 4 g, carbohydrate 25 g, fibre 7 g, cholesterol 149 mg

Chicken kebab salad

Serves 4   Preparation 1 hour 30 minutes including chilling   Cooking 10 minutes

400 g (14 oz) skinless chicken breast
  fillets
small piece fresh ginger
1 clove garlic, crushed
3 tablespoons salt-reduced soy sauce
1 tablespoon lemon juice
3 tablespoons sunflower or peanut oil
½ teaspoon sambal oelek or Chinese
  chili paste
4 small fresh red chilies
1 medium red capsicum (bell pepper)
small head baby bok choy
150 g (5 oz) mung bean sprouts

2 spring onions (scallions), thinly sliced
3 tablespoons lime juice
salt and freshly ground black pepper

PEANUT SAUCE
3 tablespoons crunchy or smooth
  peanut butter
1 teaspoon soft brown sugar
1 can (165 ml/6 fl oz) light coconut
  milk
1 tablespoon white wine vinegar
2 tablespoons salt-reduced soy sauce
½ teaspoon sambal oelek

1 Cut chicken breast fillets into large cubes. Peel ginger and grate finely. Combine ginger, garlic, soy sauce, lemon juice, 1 tablespoon oil and sambal oelek in a bowl. Add chicken and turn to coat. Chill, covered, 1 hour.

2 To make chili flowers, using a sharp knife, make 6 cuts from the stem to the tip of each chili; do not cut through the base. Place chilies in a bowl of iced water until ready to serve.

3 Halve capsicum and cut into thin strips. Cut bok choy into thin strips. Arrange capsicum, bok choy, mung beans and spring onions in serving bowls. Whisk lime juice with remaining 2 tablespoons oil. Add salt and pepper to taste. Drizzle over vegetables.

4 Preheat grill (broiler) or barbecue to medium–high heat. Remove chicken from marinade and thread onto 12 skewers. Cook chicken about 6 minutes, turning occasionally. To make peanut sauce, place all ingredients in a pan over low heat. Cook 5 minutes or until sauce thickens.

5 Place kebabs on top of salad. Coat with peanut sauce, serving remainder separately. Remove chilies from iced water and add to salad.

PER SERVING kilojoules 2170, protein 42 g, total fat 32 g, saturated fat 9 g, carbohydrate 13 g, fibre 6 g, cholesterol 85 mg

Chicken liver and apple salad

Serves 4   Preparation 1 hour 30 minutes including chilling   Cooking 10 minutes

400 g (14 oz) ready-to-cook chicken livers
½ cup (125 ml/4 fl oz) dry red wine
2 tablespoons balsamic vinegar
1 bay leaf
1 sprig thyme
1 small head oak leaf lettuce
3 tablespoons vegetable oil
2 medium onions, sliced into thin rings
2 medium tart apples
1 tablespoon butter
1 tablespoon lemon juice
3 tablespoons dry white wine
pinch of ground aniseed
1 tablespoon sultanas (golden raisins)
salt and freshly ground black pepper

1 Place chicken livers in a bowl. Add red wine, 1 tablespoon vinegar, bay leaf and thyme. Chill, covered, 1 hour.

2 Tear lettuce into small pieces and arrange on a serving plate. Heat 2 tablespoons oil in a nonstick pan. Add onions; fry until golden brown. Remove from pan; keep warm.

3 Peel apples and slice thinly. Heat butter in a saucepan over medium heat, add apple slices and cook briefly. Add lemon juice, wine, ground aniseed and sultanas. Cover pan; cook another 3 minutes or until apples have softened but still hold their shape. Remove from heat.

4 Remove chicken livers from bowl with a slotted spoon, reserving marinade. Pat livers dry on paper towels. Heat remaining 1 tablespoon oil in a nonstick pan over high heat and cook chicken livers on all sides, 2 to 3 minutes. Add salt and pepper to taste. Place chicken livers on top of lettuce.

5 Pour reserved marinade into pan and bring to a boil. Add remaining 1 tablespoon vinegar and salt and pepper to taste. Drizzle over salad. Top with apples and onions.

PER SERVING kilojoules 1611, protein 28 g, total fat 24 g, saturated fat 6 g, carbohydrate 13 g, fibre 3 g, cholesterol 639 mg

Turkey and mushroom salad

Serves **6**   Preparation **10 minutes**   Cooking **15 minutes**

250 g (8 oz) turkey or chicken tenderloins
2 tablespoons butter
salt and freshly ground black pepper
12 large white mushrooms
½ cup (125 ml/4 fl oz) dry white wine
1 bay leaf
1 sprig rosemary
2 tablespoons vegetable oil
3 tablespoons raspberry vinegar
2 tablespoons crème fraîche or sour cream
1 head oak leaf lettuce
125 g (4 oz) fresh raspberries

1 Cut turkey into small pieces. Heat 1 tablespoon butter in a nonstick pan over medium heat. Add turkey; cook 2 to 3 minutes or until golden and cooked through. Season with salt and pepper; transfer to a plate.

2 Wipe mushrooms with paper towels. Discard stalks. Heat remaining 1 tablespoon butter in pan over medium heat. Add mushrooms, open side up, and cook 3 minutes. Add wine, bay leaf, rosemary and a generous grinding of pepper. Cook, covered, another 5 minutes.

3 Transfer mushrooms to a plate. Cook pan juices over high heat until reduced to one third their original volume. Discard rosemary and bay leaf and leave pan juices to cool.

4 Pour pan juices into a large bowl. Whisk in oil, vinegar and crème fraîche. Add salt and pepper to taste. Finely chop 4 lettuce leaves. Add to bowl with turkey; stir to combine.

5 Spread remaining whole lettuce leaves on serving plates. Place mushrooms on top, open sides up, and fill with turkey salad. Garnish with raspberries.

PER SERVING kilojoules 922, protein 12 g, total fat 17 g, saturated fat 7 g, carbohydrate 3 g, fibre 3 g, cholesterol 50 mg

Fish and seafood salads

Italian seafood salad

Serves 4   Preparation 30 minutes   Cooking 30 minutes

4 tablespoons lemon juice
½ cup (125 ml/4 fl oz) white wine
  vinegar
5 black peppercorns
½ teaspoon fennel seeds
½ teaspoon salt
300 g (10 oz) gutted and cleaned
  baby squid or calamari
1 kg (2 lb) mussels, scrubbed and
  debearded
1½ cups (375 ml/13 fl oz) dry white
  wine
1 bay leaf
300 g (10 oz) medium, cooked prawns
  (shrimp), peeled and deveined,
  leaving tails intact

2 celery stalks, thinly sliced
2 roma (plum) tomatoes, finely diced
1 medium red onion, finely diced
2 cloves garlic, finely chopped
3 tablespoons finely chopped fresh
  flat-leaf parsley
heart of 1 cos (romaine) lettuce

VINAIGRETTE
5 tablespoons olive oil
3 tablespoons lemon juice
pinch of cayenne pepper
salt and freshly ground black pepper

1 Bring 2 cups (500 ml/16 fl oz) water to a boil with lemon juice, vinegar, peppercorns, fennel seeds and salt. Add squid and cook over low heat until tender, about 20 minutes. Leave squid in liquid to cool.

2 Leave mussels in a bowl of cold water for 15 minutes, then strain. Discard open mussels. Rinse remaining mussels in cold water until all traces of sand are removed.

3 In a large saucepan, bring white wine and bay leaf to a boil. Add mussels, cover and cook for about 10 minutes until they open. Strain and discard any mussels that remain closed. Remove flesh from open shells. Set aside to let cool.

4 Remove squid from cooking liquid and cut into small pieces. Combine squid, mussels and prawns in a bowl. Mix in celery, tomatoes, onion, garlic and parsley. Place lettuce leaves on individual bowls or plates.

5 To make vinaigrette, whisk oil, lemon juice and cayenne pepper until combined; add salt and pepper to taste. Drizzle over salad, toss lightly and spoon onto lettuce.

PER SERVING kilojoules 2010, protein 48 g, total fat 27 g, saturated fat 4 g, carbohydrate 10 g, fibre 3 g, cholesterol 400 mg

Tabouleh with fish in lemon dressing

Serves **4**   Preparation **1 hour including standing**   Cooking **5 minutes**   Chilling **1 hour**

1 cup (180 g/7 oz) burghul
  (bulgur wheat)
300 g (10 oz) orange roughy or
  other white fish fillets
1 small lemon, thinly sliced
2 sprigs parsley
5 black peppercorns
1 medium cucumber, seeds removed,
  diced
4 spring onions (scallions), thinly
  sliced
250 g (8 oz) cherry tomatoes, halved
2 tablespoons chopped fresh
  coriander (cilantro)

2 tablespoons chopped fresh mint
2 tablespoons chopped fresh parsley
mint sprigs, for garnish

LEMON DRESSING
2 tablespoons olive oil
2 tablespoons red wine vinegar
2 tablespoons lemon juice
1 tablespoon grated lemon peel
1 teaspoon Dijon mustard
1 clove garlic, crushed
salt and freshly ground black pepper

1 Place burghul in a large heatproof bowl and add 2 cups (500 ml/16 fl oz) boiling water. Let stand 45 minutes, or until grains are tender and water has been absorbed.

2 Meanwhile, place fish fillets in a large pan, add lemon slices, parsley sprigs and peppercorns and cold water to cover. Bring to a boil. Reduce heat and simmer, covered, 5 minutes, or until fish is opaque and flakes easily.

3 Remove fish from liquid and set aside to cool. Use a fork to separate fish into large flakes.

4 Place burghul in a serving bowl and add cucumber, spring onions, tomatoes and chopped herbs. Gently mix in fish, taking care not to break it up.

5 To make lemon dressing, whisk all ingredients in a bowl. Pour dressing over salad and mix gently to combine.

6 Chill salad, covered, for 1 hour to allow flavours to develop. Check seasoning before serving and garnish with mint sprigs.

PER SERVING **kilojoules 1228, protein 18 g, total fat 11 g, saturated fat 2 g, carbohydrate 31 g, fibre 8 g, cholesterol 14 mg**

Tuna and green bean salad

Serves **4**   Preparation **15 minutes**   Cooking **20 minutes**

3 cloves garlic, peeled
250 g (8 oz) green beans, halved
6 small red potatoes (about 375 g/13 oz), halved
2 tablespoons balsamic or red wine vinegar
2 tablespoons low-fat mayonnaise
1 tablespoon olive oil
pinch of salt
½ cup (30 g/1 oz) fresh basil leaves
250 g (8 oz) cherry tomatoes, halved
1 can (425 g/15 oz) water-packed tuna, drained
6 cos (romaine) lettuce leaves
⅓ cup (50 g/2 oz) black olives, for garnish

1 Blanch garlic in a large saucepan of boiling water for 3 minutes. Transfer garlic to a food processor or blender; set aside. Add beans to boiling water and cook 4 minutes, or until crisp-tender. Remove beans, rinse under cold water and drain. Add potatoes to pan and cook 12 minutes, or until tender; drain.

2 Add vinegar, mayonnaise, oil and salt to garlic in food processor and purée. Add basil and 2 tablespoons water and purée again.

3 Transfer dressing to a large bowl. Add tomatoes, beans, potatoes and tuna, tossing to coat. Tear lettuce into small pieces. Add lettuce and toss again. Garnish with olives.

PER SERVING kilojoules 1094, protein 26 g, total fat 9 g, saturated fat 2 g, carbohydrate 19 g, fibre 5 g, cholesterol 48 mg

Roasted capsicum and tuna salad

Serves 4   Preparation 30 minutes   Cooking 15 minutes

2 red and 2 yellow capsicums (bell peppers)
1 clove garlic
1 large head green lettuce, such as lollo bionda (green coral)
4 tablespoons olive oil
2 tablespoons white balsamic vinegar
salt and freshly ground black pepper
1 can (180 g/7 oz) tuna in water, drained
1 tablespoon small capers
1 tablespoon lemon juice
½ cup (125 g/4 oz) sour cream
1 tablespoon coarsely chopped fresh parsley, for garnish

1 Preheat oven to 240°C/475°F. Place whole capsicums on aluminum foil on baking tray. Roast 15 minutes, turning halfway through, or until blackened and blistered.

2 Remove capsicums from oven. Place cloth towel soaked in cold water on top. Leave 5 minutes. Peel away skin. Cut into broad strips.

3 Cut garlic in half horizontally and rub cut surface over inside of salad bowl. Tear lettuce into small pieces. Add capsicums and lettuce to bowl.

4 To make vinaigrette, whisk 2 tablespoons oil with vinegar until combined; add salt and pepper to taste.

5 Using a fork, break tuna into small pieces in a bowl. Add capers. Whisk remaining 2 tablespoons oil, lemon juice, sour cream and salt and pepper to taste and stir into tuna.

6 Drizzle vinaigrette on capsicum strips and lettuce. Place on a platter. Add tuna mixture and sprinkle with parsley.

PER SERVING kilojoules 1384, protein 13 g, total fat 28 g, saturated fat 8 g, carbohydrate 7 g, fibre 3 g, cholesterol 46 mg

Vegetable salad with tuna

Serves **4**   Preparation **35 to 40 minutes**   Cooking **15 minutes**

1¼ cups (150 g/5 oz) frozen peas
150 g (5 oz) frozen green beans
salt
3 chilled cooked potatoes (waxy variety), unpeeled
1 yellow and 1 green capsicum (bell pepper)
1 medium white onion
2 large tomatoes
⅔ cup (100 g/4 oz) green olives stuffed with pimiento
1 small clove garlic, finely chopped
4 tablespoons mayonnaise
1 tablespoon olive oil
2 tablespoons lemon juice
freshly ground black pepper
1 can (180 g/7 oz) water-packed tuna, drained
lemon wedges, to serve

1 Bring ½ cup (125 ml/4 fl oz) water to a boil in a saucepan with ½ teaspoon salt. Add frozen peas and beans, cover and cook 5 minutes. Pour into strainer, reserving liquid. Drain vegetables and let cool.

2 Peel potatoes and cut into small cubes. Trim capsicums and cut into short strips. Slice onion into rings. Halve tomatoes, remove seeds and cut into eighths.

3 Halve olives if desired. Place olives, peas, beans, capsicum strips, onion rings, tomato wedges and diced potatoes in a serving bowl.

4 Combine garlic, mayonnaise, oil, lemon juice and 3 tablespoons of reserved vegetable cooking water. Stir together until smooth. Add salt and pepper to taste.

5 Pour mayonnaise mixture over vegetables. Flake tuna a little. Arrange on vegetables. Serve with lemon wedges.

PER SERVING kilojoules 1227, protein 16 g, total fat 14 g, saturated fat 2 g, carbohydrate 25 g, fibre 9 g, cholesterol 24 mg

Tuna and egg salad

Serves 4   Preparation 30 minutes

2 medium eggs, hard-boiled
2 medium red capsicums (bell peppers)
⅓ cup (50 g/2 oz) green olives stuffed with pimiento
1 large onion
1 small head butter (butterhead) lettuce
1 can (425 g/15 oz) tuna in oil, drained
few sprigs oregano, for garnish

HERB VINAIGRETTE
4 tablespoons olive oil
3 tablespoons sherry vinegar
1 clove garlic, crushed
salt and freshly ground black pepper
1 tablespoon each chopped fresh thyme, oregano and flat-leaf parsley

1 Peel hard-boiled eggs and slice into rounds. Dice capsicums. Slice olives.
Cut onion into thin rings. Separate lettuce leaves and use to line serving plates.

2 Arrange eggs, capsicums, onion rings and olives on lettuce leaves. Flake tuna
into chunks and add to salad.

3 To make herb vinaigrette, whisk oil, vinegar, garlic and salt and pepper to taste.
Stir in chopped herbs.

4 Drizzle vinaigrette over salad. Garnish salad with oregano sprigs.

**PER SERVING kilojoules 1494, protein 27 g, total fat 25 g, saturated fat 5 g,
carbohydrate 6 g, fibre 3 g, cholesterol 154 mg**

Trout fillets with asparagus and tomato salad

Serves **4**   Preparation **30 minutes**   Cooking **20 to 25 minutes**

1 kg (2 lb) medium to thick green and white asparagus
1 teaspoon sugar
150 g (5 oz) cherry tomatoes, halved
400 g (14 oz) smoked trout fillets
4 small eggs, hard-boiled
3 tablespoons sunflower oil
2 tablespoons herb vinegar
1 tablespoon lemon juice
½ teaspoon grated horseradish, from a jar
salt and freshly ground black pepper
4 tablespoons light sour cream
1 tablespoon red caviar (salmon roe)
2 tablespoons chopped fresh chives, for garnish

1 Trim ends from asparagus spears. Peel white asparagus from tips to ends and green asparagus only at ends. Bring plenty of lightly salted water to a boil with sugar. Cook white asparagus 10 minutes; add green asparagus and cook a further 5 to 10 minutes. Drain asparagus; let cool.

2 Arrange asparagus and cherry tomatoes on individual plates. Cut trout fillets into large pieces and add to plates. Peel eggs; cut into quarters.

3 Whisk oil, herb vinegar, lemon juice and horseradish until combined; add salt and pepper to taste. Drizzle over salad and trout.

4 Stir sour cream until creamy, season with salt and pepper. Spoon onto each salad portion. Garnish with caviar, eggs and chives.

PER SERVING kilojoules 1846, protein 39 g, total fat 29 g, saturated fat 7 g, carbohydrate 7 g, fibre 5 g, cholesterol 291 mg

Prawn and mango salad

Serves **4**   Preparation **25 minutes**

½ medium telegraph (English) cucumber
1 medium red capsicum (bell pepper), sliced
250 g (8 oz) cherry tomatoes, quartered
2 large mangoes, peeled and sliced
16 cooked king prawns (large shrimp), peeled and
    deveined, leaving tails intact
150 g (5 oz) mixed salad leaves
1 clove garlic, crushed
1 tablespoon chili sauce
2 tablespoons olive oil
4 tablespoons lime juice
3 tablespoons chopped fresh mint
freshly ground black pepper

1 Slice cucumber into thin rounds, leaving skin on. Combine cucumber, capsicum, tomatoes, mangoes, prawns and salad leaves in a large bowl.

2 To make dressing, combine garlic, chili sauce, oil, lime juice and mint in a small screw-top jar. Shake well. Stir dressing into salad.

3 Pile salad onto individual serving plates. Season with freshly ground pepper.

PER SERVING kilojoules 1022, protein 18 g, total fat 11 g, saturated fat 2 g, carbohydrate 19 g, fibre 4 g, cholesterol 120 mg

Crisp seafood salad with yogurt dressing

1 medium head iceberg lettuce
50 g (2 oz) sorrel or baby spinach leaves
250 g (8 oz) cherry tomatoes
150 g (5 oz) cooked and peeled prawns (shrimp), thawed if frozen
4 sprigs dill, for garnish
4 thin lemon slices, for garnish

VINAIGRETTE
2 tablespoons canola or olive oil
2 tablespoons lemon juice
salt and ground white pepper

YOGURT DRESSING
1 cup (250 g/8 oz) yogurt
2 tablespoons mayonnaise
1 teaspoon dry vermouth
1 tablespoon lime juice
salt and ground white pepper
pinch of cayenne pepper

1 Cut lettuce into strips. Tear larger sorrel leaves into pieces. Arrange lettuce and sorrel on serving plates. Cut tomatoes into quarters and add to salad.

2 To make vinaigrette, whisk oil and lemon juice until combined; add salt and pepper to taste. Drizzle over lettuce.

3 To make yogurt dressing, stir yogurt, mayonnaise, vermouth and lime juice until creamy. Season well with salt, white pepper and cayenne pepper.

4 Spoon yogurt dressing and prawns on to salad. Garnish with dill and lemon slices.

PER SERVING kilojoules 930, protein 13 g, total fat 15 g, saturated fat 3 g, carbohydrate 7 g, fibre 4 g, cholesterol 84 mg

Crab and grapefruit salad

Serves **4**   Preparation **25 minutes**

4 medium grapefruit
2 tablespoons mayonnaise
1 tablespoon finely chopped mango chutney
2 teaspoons Dijon mustard
1 teaspoon sesame oil
salt and freshly ground black pepper
400 g (14 oz) crabmeat, picked over to remove any pieces of shell or cartilage
1 head witlof (Belgian endive/chicory), cut crosswise into thin strips
100 g (4 oz) watercress, tough stems trimmed
1 head lettuce, such as mignonette, separated into leaves, for serving

1 Remove skin and white pith from grapefruit with a paring knife. Working over a bowl, separate grapefruit segments from membranes; reserve juice.

2 Whisk mayonnaise, chutney, mustard, sesame oil, a pinch of salt and pepper and 3 tablespoons reserved grapefruit juice in a medium bowl.

3 Dice crab and stir into mayonnaise mixture. Add witlof, grapefruit segments and watercress and toss to combine. Serve crab salad on a bed of lettuce leaves.

PER SERVING kilojoules 765, protein 16 g, total fat 5 g, saturated fat 1 g, carbohydrate 16 g, fibre 3 g, cholesterol 87 mg

Scallops and grapefruit with mustard vinaigrette

Serves **4**   Preparation **20 minutes**   Cooking **5 minutes**

1 medium red onion
½ head curly endive (frisée) lettuce
100 g (4 oz) rocket (arugula)
2 medium pink grapefruit
12 shelled scallops with coral
2 tablespoons lemon juice
salt and freshly ground black pepper
1 tablespoon butter
2 tablespoons dry vermouth

MUSTARD VINAIGRETTE
3 tablespoons olive oil
2 tablespoons red wine vinegar
1 teaspoon wholegrain mustard
1 teaspoon honey
salt and freshly ground black pepper

1 Finely dice onion. Tear lettuce into bite-sized pieces. Remove hard stems from rocket. With a sharp knife, remove skin and white pith from grapefruit. Separate grapefruit into segments.

2 Drizzle scallops with lemon juice and sprinkle with salt and pepper. Heat butter in a nonstick pan and cook scallops about 2 minutes on each side; add vermouth and cook another 1 to 2 minutes. Remove from heat.

3 To make vinaigrette, whisk oil, vinegar, mustard and honey, until thickened slightly; add salt and pepper to taste.

4 Arrange lettuce leaves on individual plates and drizzle with vinaigrette. Top with diced onion and grapefruit segments. Arrange scallops on top.

PER SERVING kilojoules 1083, protein 10 g, total fat 19 g, saturated fat 5 g, carbohydrate 9 g, fibre 2 g, cholesterol 34 mg

Barbecued calamari with tomato vinaigrette

Serves 4   Preparation 2 hours 30 minutes including marinating   Cooking 3 minutes

500 g (1 lb) calamari or squid rings
2 cloves garlic, crushed
4 tablespoons finely chopped fresh flat-leaf parsley
2 tablespoons olive oil
4 tablespoons white wine
salt and freshly ground black pepper
1 small head cos (romaine) lettuce

TOMATO VINAIGRETTE
2 large tomatoes
2 tablespoons olive oil
1 tablespoon champagne vinegar
2 tablespoons lemon juice
4 sprigs fresh thyme, finely chopped
salt and freshly ground pepper

1 Place calamari, garlic and parsley in a bowl. Add oil, wine, salt and pepper. Mix together, cover and marinate in refrigerator about 2 hours.

2 Tear lettuce into pieces and arrange on individual plates. Halve tomatoes, remove seeds and finely dice.

3 To make tomato vinaigrette, whisk oil, champagne vinegar, lemon juice and thyme until combined; add salt and pepper to taste. Add diced tomatoes and mix together. Drizzle vinaigrette over lettuce leaves.

4 Heat barbecue or preheat grill (broiler) to medium heat. Cook calamari on barbecue or under grill about 3 minutes, turning occasionally. Place on salad and serve while hot.

PER SERVING kilojoules 1218, protein 32 g, total fat 16 g, saturated fat 3 g, carbohydrate 3 g, fibre 3 g, cholesterol 361 mg

White fish salad with olive vinaigrette

Serves 4 Preparation 35 minutes Cooking 5 to 8 minutes

500 g (1 lb) blue-eye cod or other firm white fish fillets
1 tablespoon olive oil
½ teaspoon black peppercorns
1 sprig rosemary, 2 sprigs oregano, 2 sprigs thyme and 1 bay leaf
    tied in a bunch
1 small lemon, thinly sliced
3 large tomatoes
6 marinated artichoke hearts
4 tablespoons finely chopped fresh flat-leaf parsley

OLIVE VINAIGRETTE
1 tablespoon olive oil
1 tablespoon balsamic vinegar
1 tablespoon lemon juice
2 cloves garlic, finely chopped
15 pitted green olives and 15 pitted black olives, finely chopped
½ teaspoon dried thyme
½ teaspoon dried oregano
salt and freshly ground black pepper

1 Cut fish fillets into small pieces. Brush a steamer basket with oil and add fish. Place peppercorns, bunch of herbs and lemon slices in a large saucepan.

2 Pour in water to a depth of about two fingers, taking care water does not touch fish in steamer basket. Insert steamer basket and bring water to a boil. Cover fish and cook 5 to 8 minutes, depending on its thickness. Remove steamer basket from saucepan and let fish pieces cool in it.

3 Halve tomatoes, remove seeds and slice into rounds. Cut artichokes into small pieces. Arrange tomatoes, artichokes, parsley and fish pieces on a large platter.

4 To make olive vinaigrette, whisk oil, vinegar, lemon juice and garlic until combined. Fold in olives and herbs; add salt and pepper to taste. Drizzle over salad.

PER SERVING kilojoules 983, protein 16 g, total fat 12 g, saturated fat 2 g, carbohydrate 14 g, fibre 4 g, cholesterol 41 mg

KIWIFRUIT AND BLUEBERRY SALAD

MIXED FRUIT SALAD IN MELON HALVES

WARM SUMMER FRUIT SALAD WITH SABAYON

SPICED SEASONAL FRUIT SALAD

Dessert fruit salads

FLAMBÉED APPLE AND WALNUT SALAD

TROPICAL FRUIT SALAD

MELON SALAD WITH YOGURT LIME SAUCE

VANILLA RHUBARB WITH STRAWBERRIES

DRIED FRUIT SALAD

Kiwifruit and blueberry salad

Serves **4**   Preparation **15 minutes**   Cooking **5 minutes**

½ cup (55 g/2 oz) slivered almonds
8 kiwifruit
½ cup (125 ml/4 fl oz) port or red wine
few small strips lemon peel
250 g (8 oz) blueberries
icing (confectioners') sugar, for garnish

RASPBERRY CREAM
150 g (5 oz) frozen raspberries, thawed
4 tablespoons icing (confectioners') sugar
2 teaspoons vanilla sugar
2 tablespoons raspberry liqueur (schnapps) or almond liqueur
½ cup (125 g/4 oz) double (heavy) cream

1 Dry roast slivered almonds in a pan over medium heat until golden, tossing to prevent burning. Transfer to a plate and leave to cool. Peel kiwifruit and slice crosswise.

2 Place port and lemon peel in a pan. Bring to a boil; add kiwifruit. Reduce heat to low. Poach fruit 1 minute. Remove pan from heat. Remove fruit with a slotted spoon, discarding lemon peel, and leave to cool. Arrange on serving plates with blueberries.

3 To make raspberry cream, place raspberries in a fine sieve over a bowl. Press berries with the back of a spoon to make a fine purée without any seeds. Reserve a little purée for decoration. Stir icing sugar, vanilla sugar and raspberry liqueur into purée. Fold in cream.

4 Dust kiwifruit and blueberries with icing sugar. Spoon a little raspberry cream onto plates. Using a teaspoon, swirl in a little reserved purée. Scatter on roasted slivered almonds.

PER SERVING kilojoules 2074, protein 6 g, total fat 25 g, saturated fat 11 g, carbohydrate 49 g, fibre 10 g, cholesterol 50 mg

Mixed fruit salad in melon halves

250 g (8 oz) sweet cherries
1 medium banana
4 apricots
250 g (8 oz) damsons or other blue plums
3 tablespoons lemon juice
4 tablespoons liquid honey
3 sprigs mint
2 small cantaloupe (muskmelon) or honeydew melons
½ cup (125 g/4 oz) whipping cream
mint leaves, for garnish

1 Remove pits from cherries. Slice banana, apricots and plums. Combine fruit in a bowl.

2 Mix lemon juice and honey and pour over fruit. Remove mint leaves from sprigs. Cut into fine strips. Stir into salad.

3 Halve melons and scrape out seeds. Use a melon baller to scoop out flesh, leaving a rim of flesh about 1 cm (½ inch) thick. Add melon balls to bowl.

4 Whip cream until stiff. Spoon fruit salad into melon halves. Garnish with cream rosettes and mint leaves.

PER SERVING kilojoules 1487, protein 4 g, total fat 12 g, saturated fat 8 g, carbohydrate 58 g, fibre 7 g, cholesterol 36 mg

Warm summer fruit salad with sabayon

Serves **6**   Preparation **10 minutes**   Cooking **30 minutes**

1½ cups (375 ml/13 fl oz) apple juice
2 teaspoons caster (superfine) sugar
2 tablespoons brandy
2 large peaches, halved, stoned, thickly sliced
2 large nectarines, halved, stoned, thickly sliced
2 mangoes, peeled, thickly sliced

SABAYON SAUCE
3 egg yolks
4 tablespoons caster (superfine) sugar
½ cup (125 ml/4 fl oz) brandy, rum or orange-flavoured liqueur

1 Pour apple juice into a shallow saucepan or frying pan with a lid. Add caster sugar and brandy. Bring mixture to a boil; reduce heat to medium.

2 Add peaches and nectarines to pan. Cover and poach gently 2 minutes. If skins come off, remove from pan. Add mangoes and poach another 2 minutes. Transfer to a serving bowl, using a slotted spoon.

3 Boil juice mixture 5 to 10 minutes, or until reduced to a slightly heavy syrup. Pour over fruit.

4 To make sabayon sauce, beat egg yolks and caster sugar in top half of a double boiler over gently simmering water, 2 to 3 minutes, until creamy.

5 Beating continuously, add brandy in a thin, steady stream. Continue beating 10 to 12 minutes until sauce is thick. Pour into a jug and serve with poached fruit.

PER SERVING kilojoules 1040, protein 3 g, total fat 3 g, saturated fat 1 g, carbohydrate 38 g, fibre 4 g, cholesterol 106 mg

Spiced seasonal fruit salad

Serves **6**   Preparation **20 minutes**   Chilling **2 hours or overnight**

1 large mango, peeled and sliced
250 g (8 oz) cherries, pitted
⅔ cup (100 g/4 oz) seedless green grapes
250 g (8 oz) strawberries, hulled and cut in half
3 large apricots, halved, stoned, sliced
¾ cup (55 g/2 oz) desiccated (dried) coconut
1 tablespoon caster (superfine) sugar
generous pinch of cayenne pepper
generous pinch of mustard powder
pinch of salt

1 Place all the fruit in a large serving bowl.

2 Finely grind coconut in a spice mill or with a pestle and mortar. Add remaining ingredients and mix well.

3 Add spiced coconut mixture to fruit and stir well to combine. Cover and refrigerate at least 2 hours, preferably overnight to allow the flavours to blend and develop.

PER SERVING kilojoules 580, protein 2 g, total fat 6 g, saturated fat 5 g, carbohydrate 18 g, fibre 4 g, cholesterol 0 mg

Flambéed apple and walnut salad

6 medium tart apples (such as granny smith or boskoop)
2 tablespoons lemon juice
½ cup (125 ml/4 fl oz) dry white wine
1 tablespoon soft brown sugar
2 tablespoons raisins
1 vanilla bean
2 tablespoons crème fraîche or light sour cream
½ cup (55 g/2 oz) walnuts
3 tablespoons Calvados (apple brandy), cognac or dark rum

1 Quarter and peel apples and remove seeds. Cut quarters into large pieces. Place apple pieces, lemon juice, wine, brown sugar and raisins in a saucepan.

2 Slit open vanilla bean and scrape out seeds. Add seeds and bean to pan. Bring mixture to a boil. Cover and cook over low heat 4 to 5 minutes. Apples should be soft but still hold their shape.

3 Remove pan from heat. Remove vanilla bean and drain apples, reserving liquid. Stir crème fraîche into liquid and spoon onto serving plates.

4 Coarsely chop walnuts. Mix with apples and distribute among serving plates.

5 Flambé a little Calvados for each salad portion: Heat Calvados over low heat in a small saucepan; scoop a little into a ladle, ignite the alcohol with a long match or lighter, and pour flaming alcohol over fruit salad, one serving at a time. Serve at once.

PER SERVING kilojoules 1287, protein 3 g, total fat 14 g, saturated fat 4 g, carbohydrate 35 g, fibre 5 g, cholesterol 13 mg

Tropical fruit salad

Serves 4   Preparation 30 minutes

4 tablespoons apricot nectar
2 tablespoons lime juice
3 tablespoons chopped fresh mint leaves
1 large ripe but firm mango, peeled and
    cut into chunks
2 medium slices fresh or canned pineapple,
    cut into wedges
1 large banana, thickly sliced
2 kiwifruit, peeled and cut into chunks
1 medium pawpaw or large papaya, peeled,
    seeded and cut into chunks

1 Whisk apricot nectar, lime juice and mint in a large bowl.
Add mango, pineapple, banana and kiwifruit, tossing to combine.
Refrigerate until serving time.

2 To serve, add pawpaw and toss again.

**PER SERVING kilojoules 594, protein 3 g, total fat 0 g, saturated fat 0 g,
carbohydrate 31 g, fibre 7 g, cholesterol 0 mg**

Melon salad with yogurt lime sauce

Serves **8** Preparation **30 minutes**

¼ small watermelon (1 kg/2 lb), cubed
½ cantaloupe (muskmelon), cubed (about 2½ cups)
¼ honeydew melon, cubed (2 cups)
1 cup (175 g/6 oz) seedless red or green grapes
½ small pineapple (500 g/1 lb), cubed

YOGURT LIME SAUCE
1 cup (250 g/8 oz) yogurt
2 tablespoons sour cream
2 tablespoons honey
1 tablespoon lime juice
pinch of ground ginger

1 Combine all the melons, grapes and pineapple in a large bowl. Chill, covered, until serving time.

2 To make yogurt lime sauce, combine yogurt, sour cream, honey, lime juice and ginger in a small bowl. Chill, covered, until serving time.

3 Serve fruit salad in individual bowls. Serve yogurt lime sauce on the side.

PER SERVING kilojoules 623, protein 3 g, total fat 4 g, saturated fat 2 g, carbohydrate 26 g, fibre 3 g, cholesterol 12 mg

Vanilla rhubarb with strawberries

800 g (1 lb 12 oz) thin rhubarb stalks
1 vanilla bean
⅔ cup (160 ml/6 fl oz) dry white wine
3 to 4 tablespoons granulated sugar
500 g (1 lb) strawberries
2 tablespoons orange liqueur
1 tablespoon icing (confectioners') sugar

1 Peel rhubarb stalks and cut into small pieces.

2 Split open vanilla bean lengthwise and scrape out seeds. Cut in half crosswise. Place rhubarb, vanilla pod, vanilla seeds, wine and sugar in a saucepan and bring to a boil.

3 Cook rhubarb, covered, over low heat 4 to 5 minutes. The pieces should still hold their shape and not become very soft. Remove from heat, let rhubarb cool. Refrigerate 1 hour.

4 Remove vanilla bean and spoon rhubarb into small bowls. Cut about two-thirds of the strawberries into pieces and place in a food processor with orange liqueur and icing sugar. Purée until a strawberry froth forms on the surface.

5 Pour puréed strawberries over rhubarb pieces. Garnish each portion with remaining strawberries.

PER SERVING kilojoules 655, protein 4 g, total fat 0 g, saturated fat 0 g, carbohydrate 29 g, fibre 6 g, cholesterol 0 mg

Dried fruit salad

Serves **6**   Preparation **1 hour including chilling**   Cooking **25 minutes**

1¼ cups (225 g/8 oz) pitted prunes
1 cup (135 g/5 oz) dried apricots
¾ cup (125 g/4 oz) dried peaches or pears, halved
⅓ cup (55 g/2 oz) sultanas (golden raisins)
few thin strips orange peel
1 vanilla bean, halved
½ cup (100 g/4 oz) sugar
2 tablespoons orange flower water or rose water
1 cup (250 g/8 oz) low-fat yogurt, to serve

1 Place prunes, apricots, peaches, sultanas and orange peel strips in a large saucepan with 4 cups (1 litre/2 pints) water. Scrape seeds from vanilla bean; add seeds and bean to pan. Partly cover and bring slowly to a boil.

2 Cover and simmer 5 minutes. Add sugar and stir until dissolved. Cover and simmer over low heat another 15 minutes; allow to cool.

3 Drain, transfer to a serving bowl with a little juice from the pan. Stir in orange flower water. Refrigerate, covered, 1 hour. Serve with yogurt on the side.

PER SERVING kilojoules 1143, protein 6 g, total fat 0.5 g, saturated fat 0 g, carbohydrate 62 g, fibre 7 g, cholesterol 2 mg

Index

Healthy Salads

Editorial Project Manager Deborah Nixon
Designer Avril Makula
Proofreader Susan McCreery
Indexer Diane Harriman
Production Manager – Books Susan Maffucci
Senior Production Controller Monique Tesoriero

READER'S DIGEST GENERAL BOOKS
Editorial Director Elaine Russell
Managing Editor Rosemary McDonald
Art Director Carole Orbell

Healthy Salads is published by
Reader's Digest (Australia) Pty Limited
80 Bay Street, Ultimo NSW 2007
www.readersdigest.com.au
www.readersdigest.co.nz
www.readersdigest.co.za

First published 2009. Reprinted 2010.
Copyright © Reader's Digest (Australia) Pty Limited 2009
Copyright © Reader's Digest Association Far East Limited 2009 Philippines
Copyright © Reader's Digest Association Far East Limited 2009

Material in this book was originally published in *Super Salads*,
Reader's Digest (Australia) Pty Limited, 2008

National Library of Australia Cataloguing-in-Publication data:

Healthy salads.
ISBN: 978-1-921569-11-1 (pbk.)
Includes index.
1. Cookery. 2. Salads.
I. Reader's Digest (Australia).
614.83

Prepress by Sinnott Bros, Sydney
Printed and bound by Leo Paper Products Ltd, China

We are interested in receiving your comments on the contents of this book. Write to: The Editor,
General Books Editorial, Reader's Digest (Australia) Pty Limited, GPO Box 4353, Sydney, NSW 2001,
or email us at bookeditors.au@readersdigest.com

To order additional copies of *Healthy Salads*, please contact us as follows:
www.readersdigest.com.au, 1300 300 030 (Australia);
www.readersdigest.co.nz, 0800 400 060 (New Zealand);
www.readersdigest.co.za, 0800 980 572 (South Africa)
or email us at customerservice@au.readersdigest.com

Product code: 041 3817